CAMBRIDGE

COMPACT

KEY
FOR SCHOOLS
SECOND EDITION

WITH ONLINE
PRACTICE

A2

STUDENT'S BOOK
WITHOUT ANSWERS

Emma Heyderman and Susan White

For the revised exam from 2020

Cambridge University Press
www.cambridge.org/elt

Cambridge Assessment English
www.cambridgeenglish.org

Information on this title: www.cambridge.org/ 9781108348744

First published 2014
Second edition 2019

20 19 18 17 16

Printed in Malaysia by Vivar Printing

A catalogue record for this publication is available from the British Library

ISBN 978-1-108-34874-4 Student's Book without answers with Online Practice

The publishers have no responsibility for the persistence or accuracy
of URLs for external or third-party internet websites referred to in this publication,
and do not guarantee that any content on such websites is, or will remain,
accurate or appropriate. Information regarding prices, travel timetables, and other
factual information given in this work is correct at the time of first printing but
the publishers do not guarantee the accuracy of such information thereafter.

Contents

MAP OF THE UNITS

UNIT	TOPICS	GRAMMAR	VOCABULARY	FUNCTIONS
1 My family, my friends & me	People Daily life	*have got* Present simple Question words	Family Daily activities Describing people	Talking about routines and habits Asking for and telling the time Describing everyday activities
2 In my free time	Hobbies & leisure Personal opinions	Adverbs of frequency *Do you like …? / Would you like …?*	Free-time activities	Expressing preferences, likes and dislikes Giving and responding to invitations
3 Eating in, eating out	House & home Food & drink	*There is / are, a / an, some & any* *(don't) have to*	House & furniture Food & drink	Saying where things are Describing food Ordering food Expressing obligation
4 What are you doing now?	Sport Clothes	Present continuous Present continuous vs present simple	Sport Clothes	Talking about what people are doing now Describing what people are wearing
5 Great places to visit	Places & buildings Time	Past simple *ago* Time expressions: *in / at / on*	Places Days & dates	Describing places Talking about dates Talking about events in the past
6 Getting there	Transport Travel	Comparative adjectives Superlative adjectives	Transport Travel	Making comparisons
7 School rules!	Education Entertainment	*must / mustn't* *should / shouldn't* *can / could* Adverbs of manner	Education Musical instruments	Expressing rules and obligation Giving advice Talking about ability in the present and past
8 We had a great time!	Holidays Personal experiences	Past continuous Past simple & past continuous	Holiday activities Adjectives of opinion	Talking about events in progress in the past Giving opinions
9 What's on?	Entertainment & media Television	*be going to* Infinitives & *-ing* forms	Going out TV programmes Word-building	Making suggestions Talking about future plans
10 Are you an outdoors person?	The natural world Weather	*will / won't & may* First conditional	The countryside Weather & seasons	Following instructions Making predictions about the future Expressing certainty and doubt
11 Healthy body, healthy mind	Health & illness Personal feelings	Present perfect *just* *yet / already* Present perfect with *for & since*	The body Health & illness Adjectives	Talking about recent past events Talking about health problems Discussing personal feelings
12 Technology & me	Communication Appliances	The passive: present simple The passive: past simple	Communication & technology Describing objects	Describing simple objects Checking understanding

READING	WRITING	LISTENING	SPEAKING
Part 2: Three texts about family	Part 7: Story	Part 3: A conversation about a school day	Part 1: Describing people
Part 3: An interview with a teenage painter	Part 5: Completing an email about a boy's family, friends and hobbies	Part 4: Five short conversations	Part 1: Asking and answering about free time
Part 4: An article about a boy from Mali	Part 7: Story	Part 2: A talk about a school trip to a school of cooking	Part 2: Asking and answering about meals
Part 1: Notices and messages	Part 6: An email about clothes	Part 1: Five short conversations	Part 2: Asking and answering about clothes and fashion
Part 2: Three texts about a school trip	Part 6: An email about a shopping trip	Part 2: Information about a Hollywood tour	Part 1: Questions about things you did this week
Part 3: An article about a teenage inventor	Part 5: An email about a trip to San Francisco	Part 5: A conversation about getting to a birthday party	Part 2: Asking and answering about means of transport
Part 1: Notices	Part 6: An email about school	Part 2: A talk by a new teacher	Part 1: Questions about school subjects
Part 4: An article about a holiday in Guadeloupe	Part 7: Story	Part 5: A conversation about where friends stayed on holiday	Part 2: Asking and answering about holidays
Part 3: An article about a teenager's unusual life	Part 6: A message to a friend about a show	Part 4: Five short conversations	Part 1: Questions about plans for the evening and a holiday
Part 1: Notices and messages	Part 7: Story	Part 1: Five short conversations	Part 2: Asking and answering about outdoor activities
Part 4: An article about the history of glasses Part 2: Three texts about staying in hospital	Part 6: An email about keeping fit	Part 3: A conversation about a Healthy Living Day	Part 1: Questions about yourself
Part 2: Three texts about teenagers and computers	Part 5: Completing emails about a lost phone	Part 5: A conversation about favourite things	Part 2: Asking and answering about technology

1 My family, my friends & me

FAMILY

Have you got an unusual family?

Tim: Yes! I've got the same name as my dad and his dad. It's Tim Alex Brown.

Mathilde: Yes, I have. I've got the same birthday as my sister, my mum and her sister. It's 3 March.

Emin: I think so. I've got a twin* brother and we've got two sisters. They're also twins!

*twin: one of two children who are born to the same mother at the same time

Grammar

Grammar – have got

» Page 90

1 Read the information about Tim, Mathilde and Emin. Are the sentences true (T) or false (F)?

1 Emin hasn't got any brothers or sisters.
2 Tim's grandfather is called Tim Alex Brown.
3 Mathilde's aunt's birthday is on 3 March.

2 Underline examples of *have got* and *has got* in the texts and questions in Exercise 1, then answer the questions below.

1 What word do we use to make the negative?
2 How do we make questions?
3 How do we make short answers?

3 Exam candidates often make mistakes with *have got*. Correct the mistakes in these sentences. The sentences are all in British English.

1 Her eyes are green and she gots long, black hair.
2 Please help her if she got any problems.
3 I'm got some friends. My best friend is Juan Manuel.
4 We had to move because my father gets a new job here.

4 Complete the question (Q) and answers (A) with the correct form of *have got*.

Q: (1) Have you got an interesting name?
(2) .... your friends .... unusual names?
A: No, I (3) .... (not) but I (4) .... a nickname*. It's Skater Blue because I've got a blue skateboard!
A: My best friend (5) .... a special name. It's Ace and it means 'one'. He (6) .... (not) an unusual surname, it's Roberts.
A: We (7) .... an unusual surname. It's Singh. My grandfather says it's an Indian word for 'lion'.
A: My cousins (8) .... beautiful names. Their names are Fleur and Eira. Fleur is 'flower' in French and Eira means 'snow'. It comes from Wales.

*nickname: this isn't your real name, but it's the name that your friends or family call you

Reading & Writing Part 2

1 Look at Sofia's family tree, then complete her blog post with words from the box. You'll need to make some words plural.

> aunt brother children cousin daughter
> father grandfather grandmother husband mother
> parents sister son uncle wife

Family tree (David & Lucia → Mateo, Paula, Victoria, Lucas → Sofia, Ariana, Daniela, Sara)

David — Lucia
Mateo — Paula / Victoria — Lucas
Sofia / Ariana / Daniela / Sara

💡 **Exam tip**

In Part 2, read the three texts carefully. Don't just match words in the text with the questions. A text can include words from the question and be the wrong answer.

✓ **Exam task**

For each question, choose the correct answer.

		Leo	Bastian	Callum
1	Which person has got family members in different countries?	A	B	C
2	Which person shares a bedroom with another member of his family?	A	B	C
3	Which person has got a cousin who lives near him?	A	B	C
4	Which person helps someone in his family?	A	B	C
5	Which person lives with a grandparent?	A	B	C
6	Which person enjoys spending time with one member of his family?	A	B	C
7	Which person thinks it is good to have a big family?	A	B	C

●●●

Let me tell you about my family. I've got one (1) ...... *sister* ......, Ariana, but I haven't got any brothers. Mateo and Paula are my (2) .... My mum's sister Victoria is my favourite (3) .... Her husband Lucas is my (4) .... They've got two (5) .... Daniela and Sara are our (6) .... My (7) .... is called David and his (8) .... is called Lucia. They haven't got any (9) ...., only daughters.

My family

Leo
There are a lot of us in my family, and I love it. Our house is crowded, so I'm never alone or bored. I've got a brother and three sisters. My brother and I have one bedroom, and my sisters have another. Mum and Dad work a lot, and my grandparents live near us, so they often look after us when my parents are working. My grandfather is from France, and he sometimes helps me with my French homework.

Bastian
I live with my mum, dad and brother. My brother and I have our own bedrooms. He's only a year older than me, so we do lots of things together, which is fun. We've got an aunt and uncle who live in the same street as us, together with their daughter – our cousin – and our grandparents. Dad works in an office, and Mum is a teacher. She was born in Italy, but she came to live here in the USA a long time ago.

Callum
My family is big, but we don't all live in the same place. I have cousins in Germany and Australia, so I don't see them very often. My parents, my sister and I share a house with my grandma, but my sister and I have our own bedrooms. Mum and Dad go out to work, and they don't have much free time, so sometimes I tidy up the house. Mum likes it when I do that.

Reading & Writing

Reading & Writing Part 7

✏ » Page 114

1 Read the text and complete the words.

Most teenagers have a favourite place to spend time. We asked you to send us a message about your favourite place. Here are your top five answers.

1 my b…… …… …… …… ……

2 my local p…… …… ……

3 the b…… …… …… ……

4 the s…… …… …… ……where I live

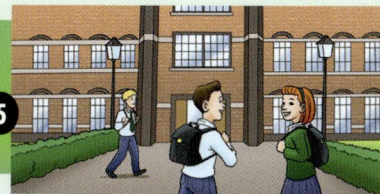

5 my s…… …… …… …… ……

2 Read the sentences below. Complete the sentences with the correct prepositions from the box.

above along between in on out of to

1 The girl and her sister sat ………………… their bedroom.
2 The family decided to go ………………… the park.
3 The girl and her friends played football ………………… the beach.
4 The boy ran ………………… the street to his friend's house.
5 At the end of the day, the children walked ………………… the school.

3 Look at picture 1 and the sentence.

A boy bought a book in a shop.

Now look at pictures 2 and 3 in the story and write about each picture.

💡 **Exam tip**

You often need to write about the places you can see in the three pictures. Remember to use the correct preposition (*in*, *at*, *to*, etc.) for each place.

✓ **Exam task**

Look at the three pictures.
Write the story shown in the pictures.
Write 35 words or more.

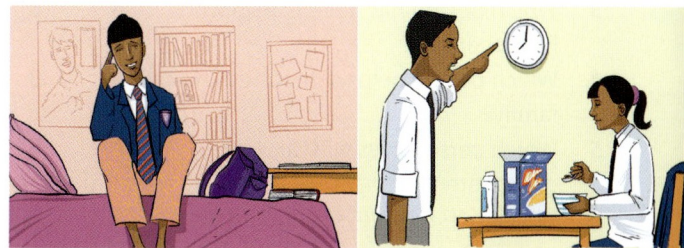

Grammar & Vocabulary

1 Work in pairs. Ask and answer questions about these times.

1 7:40
2 (clock)
3 12:55
4 (clock)
5 10:45
6 (clock)

2 Match the expressions with the pictures in Kyle's photo album.

1 have lunch   D
2 watch TV
3 do homework
4 get home
5 start school
6 walk to school
7 wake up
8 go to bed

Mobile uploads • Every day
by Kyle Walker

A — 7:30 am — 8.00
B
C
D
E
F
G
H

3 🔊 02 Listen to Kyle talking to a friend about what he does every day. Write the correct time on each picture in Kyle's photo album.

Grammar – Present simple

📝 » Page 90

4 Match the rules (1–3) with the example sentences (a–c).

1 When we use *he / she / it*, we add -s or -es to the main verb.
2 We make the negative with *don't* and *doesn't*.
3 We use *do* and *does* to make questions and short answers.

a I don't have lunch at 12 p.m. / She doesn't walk to school.
b Do you go to bed at 10 p.m.? Yes, I do. / Does he watch TV at 8 p.m.? No, he doesn't.
c He wakes up at 7.30 a.m. / She does her homework at 5 p.m.

5 🔘 Exam candidates often make mistakes with the present simple. Correct one mistake in each sentence.

1 The class starts at 2 p.m. and ~~finishs~~ at 3 p.m.   *finishes*
2 The room don't have any furniture.
3 My mother want me to be at home at 9 p.m.
4 My sister do this sport and she's very good.
5 What you think about this class?
6 It doesnt matter that you can't find the information.

6 Write sentences that are true for you. Use the present simple.

1 7.00 (I / wake up)
   I don't wake up at 7.00. I wake up at 7.30.
2 8.30 (I / walk to school with my friends)
3 9.00 (school / start)
4 12.00 (I / have lunch)
5 4.00 (my friends / do their homework)
6 6.00 (my mum / get home)
7 7.00 (we / watch TV)
8 8.30 (my best friend / go to bed)

Listening

Simon

Exam tip

Sometimes the answer is a time. Say the times in the answers quietly to yourself before you listen.

1 🔊 **03** Listen to the first part of the exam task and choose the correct times.

1 What time does Simon wake up?
  a 6.15
  b 7.00

2 What time does Simon leave home?
  a 7.00
  b 7.30

✓ Exam task

🔊 **04** **For each question, choose the correct answer. You will hear Simon talking to his friend Amanda about his school day.**

1 Amanda's tired because she
  A watches TV in bed.
  B goes to sleep very late.
  C wakes up early.

2 What time does the boat to Simon's school leave?
  A 6.15
  B 7.00
  C 7.30

3 How old is Simon?
  A 11
  B 12
  C 14

4 Simon eats his dinner
  A at his aunt's house.
  B at home.
  C at school.

5 Amanda thinks Simon's day is
  A exciting.
  B fun.
  C unusual.

Grammar – Question words

📋 » **Page 92**

2 Complete the questions with these words.

How	What	What time	When	Where	Who

1 ......Who...... is Tanya?
  a Simon's sister
  b Simon's aunt

2 .... does Simon live?
  a on an island
  b near his school

3 .... does Simon's mum wake him up?
  a 6.15
  b 7.15

4 .... does Simon go to school each day?
  a by bus
  b by boat

5 .... do children on the island change school?
  a at six years old
  b at 12 years old

6 .... does Simon do at 7 a.m.?
  a leave home
  b get on a boat

3 🔊 **04** Listen to the exam task again. Choose the correct answers to the questions in Exercise 2.

4 Write more questions. Use words from each box.

1	2
Who	you
What	your mum / brother / best friend
Where	your friends / classmates
How	
What time	
When	

3
wake up?
go to school / work?
have breakfast / lunch / dinner?
do homework?
watch TV?
do in the evening?

How does your mum go to work?

Speaking Part 1
💬 ≫ Page 119

A B C D E F

1 Work in pairs. Match the descriptions with the people in the picture.

1 Jason's my best friend. He's got short, curly hair and blue eyes. He's very tall.   F

2 My sister Lee has got brown eyes. Her hair's short and curly. She's really tall.

3 Trent's in my class. His eyes are blue. He's got straight hair and he's short.

4 Jenny's quite short. She's got long, dark, straight hair and green eyes.

2 Work in pairs. Write a description of one of your classmates but don't write his/her name.

3 Work in small groups. Take turns to read your descriptions and guess who the student is.

> He's very tall. He's got short dark hair. His eyes are blue.

> Is it Diego?

> Yes, it is!

4 🔊 05 At the end of Speaking Part 1, the examiner might ask you a *Tell me something about ...* question. Listen and complete the examiner's question.

1 Ana, tell me something about
....

2 Malik, tell me something about
....

💡 Exam tip

Try to say at least three sentences for each *Tell me something about ...* question.

5 🔊 05 Listen again. Who gives the best answer? Why?

6 Work in pairs. Write a better answer for Ana or Malik. Use the words in brackets to help you.

(What's her name?) **(1)** ....Her name's.... Mrs Reed.
(What does she look like?) **(2)** .... short dark hair and blue eyes.
(What does she do every day?) **(3)** .... to school by .... **(4)** .... lunch at school.
(Your opinion) I like her because **(5)** ....

✅ Exam task

Take turns to be the examiner and the candidate. The examiner reads the question and the candidate answers.

1 Tell me something about your school day.

2 Tell me something about your favourite teacher.

3 Tell me something about what you do at the weekend.

4 Tell me something about your best friend.

2 In my free time

Grammar & Vocabulary

📝 » Page 92

1 Complete the activities with words from the box.

collect	draw	listen	play	play
sleep	take	watch		

1 ......play...... an instrument
2 .... things
3 .... sports
4 .... pictures
5 .... photos
6 .... films
7 .... to songs
8 .... in a tent

2 Complete the messages with words from Exercise 1.

Grammar – Adverbs of frequency

We've got some great clubs in my school. I'm in the Camera Club. It's brilliant. We **usually** take (1) .... in the school but we also go to the town centre **once a month**. We **sometimes** watch (2) ...., too. I joined the Camping Club as well because I'm **often** bored at the weekend. About **four times a year**, we sleep (3) ....

I'm in the Music Club. We **always** meet **twice a week**. We listen (4) .... and we **sometimes** play an (5) .... My friends are in the Art Club and they draw (6) .... **every Monday**.

3 Look at the words in bold in the messages in Exercise 2, then complete the rules with the correct words.

1 Adverbs of frequency (e.g. *always, often*, etc.) go *before / after* the verb *be*.
2 Adverbs of frequency (e.g. *always, often*, etc.) go *before / after* all other verbs.
3 Adverbial phrases (e.g. *once a month, twice a year, every day*, etc.) can go at the *beginning and end / end* of the sentence.

4 👁 Exam candidates often make mistakes with adverbs of frequency. Find seven more mistakes in this text.

often do
My friends and I ~~do often~~ after-school activities. I'm in the Art Club. The classes are normaly on Monday and Wednesday at five o'clock. They often are 60 minutes long. My best friend is in the Cinema Club. They somtimes watch a film and talk about it. I'm not a member of that club because I don't never eat at school. My sister is in a Food Club. They ussually meet two times a month in a restaurant. Always she cooks delicious food at home.

5 Complete the sentences with the words and phrases from the box.

always	every day	~~sometimes~~	three times a week

1 When we go on holiday, my mum ...sometimes... takes photos of the hotel, but not always.
2 My sister goes to a Music Club on Tuesday, Thursday and Friday. She has a piano lesson ....
3 We always watch TV after dinner. We watch TV ....
4 My best friend wakes up at 7.55 but school starts at eight o'clock so he's .... late.

Listening Part 4

1 Work in pairs. Look at the exam task and answer the questions.

1 How many questions are there in Listening Part 4?
2 For each question, how many possible answers do you choose from?
3 Read the questions again. How many people do you think you will hear in each one (one person or two)?

2 🔊 **06** Abbey and Jasmine are talking about Abbey's favourite film star. Listen and complete these sentences from their conversation.

Jasmine: He's really good-looking, isn't he?
Abbey: Yes, he is. He's (1) .... a really good actor. That's the (2) .... I prefer him to any other actor.
Abbey: In the last few years his films (3) .... been very good.

In question 1 it says 'You will hear two friends …', so that's two people speaking.

How many questions are there in Part 4?

I can see five questions, so the answer is five.

💡 Exam tip

You will often hear words which are the same as the words in the question, or all three of the possible options, A, B, C. However, only one is the correct answer to the question.

3 Look at this exam question and the three possible options. In which parts of Abbey and Jasmine's conversation can you find A, B and C?

Why does Abbey like her favourite actor?
A He makes good films.
B He is good-looking.
C He is a good actor.

4 We know that option A is not the correct answer to the question, because of Abbey's last sentence in Exercise 2. Look at options B and C, and read what Abbey and Jasmine say again. Which is the right answer? Why?

✓ Exam task

🔊 **07** For each question, choose the correct answer.

1 You will hear two friends talking about a film they've just seen. What type of film was it?
A a comedy
B a horror film
C an adventure film

2 You will hear a boy talking about a camping trip. Who did he go camping with?
A his brother
B his mother
C his uncle

3 You will hear a boy, James, talking to his mother about basketball lessons. What does James ask his mother to do?
A find out when his basketball lessons start
B book some basketball lessons for him
C buy him some basketball clothes

4 You will hear two friends discussing a practice for their dance group. What do they still need to do?
A tell people when the practice will start
B find a place to practise
C decide on a dance

5 You will hear a girl talking about horse riding. Why does she like horse riding?
A She is learning something new.
B She can spend time outdoors.
C She has made new friends.

Grammar

Grammar – *Do you like … ?* / *Would you like … ?*

📝 **» Page 92**

1 Look at the pictures. What does Sam say about trying new food?

Does he want to join Ruby's club? Why? / Why not?

> Do you like trying new food?

> Oh yes! I love eating food from all over the world.

> Would you like to join our Cooking Club?

> No thanks! I'm not interested in cooking.

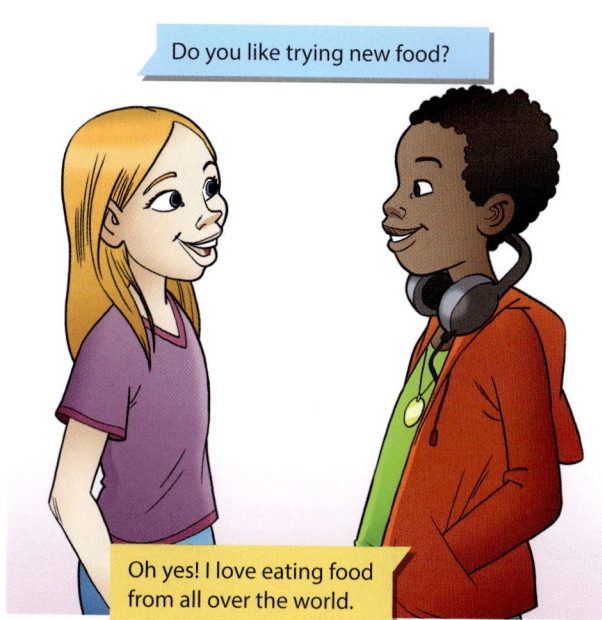

2 Complete the conversations with *Do you like* or *Would you like* and the correct form of the verb in brackets.

1 **A:** *Would you like to join* (join) our music group?
   B: I'm afraid not. I can't sing very well.

2 **A:** .... (read) books?
   B: Not really. I prefer reading blogs.

3 **A:** I'm going to the cinema. .... (come)?
   B: I'd love to.

4 **A:** I really enjoy sleeping under the stars.
   B: .... (go) camping with me next week?

5 **A:** What do you do in your free time? .... (play) sports?
   B: No, I don't. I like watching them.

6 **A:** I'm often bored on Sunday afternoon. I never know what to do.
   B: .... (watch) a film at my house this Sunday?

3 <u>Underline</u> one expression in Exercise 2 that we can use to say 'yes' to an invitation and ⭕ one expression we can use to say 'no'.

4 Complete the table with more expressions we use to say 'yes' or 'no' to invitations.

> Good idea.   I'd like to, but I can't.   I'd love to.
> I'm afraid I'm busy.   I'm afraid not.
> I'm sorry, I can't.   No, thanks.
> That's great – thanks!   Sure!   ~~Yes, please!~~

yes	no
Yes, please!	

5 Work in pairs. Take turns to invite each other to these events. Use *Would you like … ?* and the expressions in Exercise 4.

- School disco, Saturday 7.00 p.m.
- 5 km-run this summer
- Camping trip this weekend
- Visit to Science Museum tomorrow

> Would you like to go to the school disco on Saturday?

> No, thanks. I hate dancing.

Reading & Writing

Reading & Writing Part 3

1 Match the words (1–6) with the words that mean the same (a–f).

1	famous	**a**	good-looking
2	difficult	**b**	scared
3	afraid	**c**	happy
4	attractive	**d**	hard
5	correct	**e**	well-known
6	glad	**f**	right

✓ Exam task

For each question, choose the correct answer.

2 Read this text and the question below. Answer B is wrong (see underlined text). <u>Underline</u> the parts of the text where you can find answers A and C. Which is the correct answer for the question?

I'm reading a new book by my favourite writer. She's not well-known, and <u>her stories aren't easy to understand</u>, but this one is really interesting. I hope no one tells me how it ends before I finish reading it!

The boy is worried that

A the writer's stories will change now she's famous.
B this book is too difficult for him to finish.
C someone will let him know what happens in the story.

Kris Davies started painting when he was 12. He's now 15, and has a website of his own paintings. Our journalist Tamara Yafai went to meet him.

How did you become interested in painting, Kris?

It's strange. My mother's a painter – you can see her best paintings on her website – but I've never been interested in the type of paintings she does. Then, a few years ago, my sister asked me to paint a card for a friend's birthday. Her friend loved it, and I haven't stopped painting ever since.

About a year later, I decided to enter a painting competition. I wanted to use my mum's brushes, but she was using them all the time. So my uncle bought me some, which were fantastic. I came first in that competition!

Where do your ideas come from?

Seeing different places is really interesting. They help me think of new things to paint. Often I use my phone to film places I see, to help me remember them. People have given me beautiful books of paintings, but they don't help me get new ideas.

What type of painting are you interested in?

Well, all my favourite artists paint people. But I love animals and being in the countryside, so I hope to be a painter of nature. I've tried painting buildings. That was too hard for me.

Do you have any advice for other young painters?

The best painters never stop painting. That's how they become so good, and it's how you will get better. Also, remember to ask other people what they think of your paintings – even if you don't like what they say.

---

1 How did Kris first become interested in painting?
  A He saw some interesting paintings online.
  B A member of his family is a painter.
  C He painted something for a friend.

2 How did Kris get his first brushes?
  A He won them.
  B They were a present.
  C They belonged to his mother.

3 Kris gets his ideas from
  A films.
  B places he visits.
  C books about paintings.

4 Kris wants to paint
  A people.
  B buildings.
  C nature.

5 Kris says that other young painters should
  A do lots of painting.
  B look at the paintings that the best artists paint.
  C not worry about other people's opinions of their paintings.

Speaking

Speaking Part 1
💬 » Page 119

1 Complete the table with expressions we use to talk about the free-time activities we like and don't like.

> be bad at   be brilliant at
> be good at   be interested in   be terrible at
> don't like   enjoy   hate   like   love   prefer

positive ☺	negative ☹
be good at	hate

2 Complete the sentences about your free-time activities. Use the words from the box or your own ideas.

> cooking   dancing   going to concerts
> messaging friends   playing computer games
> reading books   trying new food

1 I love _trying new food_, but I don't like _cooking_.
2 I'm good at ....
  but I'm terrible at ....
3 I'm interested in ....
  but I'm not interested in ....
4 I enjoy ...., but
  I hate ....
5 I prefer ....
  to ....

3 Work in pairs. Ask and answer questions about the activities in Exercise 2.

4 In the second part of Speaking Part 1, the examiner may ask you about your free time. Complete the examiner's questions in this conversation.

Examiner: Now, let's talk about weekends. What sports _do you_ play _at the_ weekend?
Candidate: I'm sorry, I don't understand.
Examiner: (1) ....
  football at the weekend?
Candidate: No. I play volleyball.
Examiner: Who (2) ....
  time with at the weekend?
Candidate: I spend time with my friends.

5 🔊 08 Listen and check your answers.

6 Work in pairs. Improve the candidate's answers in Exercise 4.

I spend a lot of time with my friends at the weekend. We go shopping or play computer games.

✓ Exam task

Student A, you are the examiner. Ask the examiner's questions in Exercise 4.

Student B, you are the candidate. Answer the examiner's questions with true information about you. Remember to say as much as you can.

Reading & Writing Part 5

1 ⊙ Exam candidates often make mistakes with pronouns.
Write the correct pronoun in each space.

1 I like my bedroom and the dining room because ......*they*...... are big.
2 Because .... is summer here the weather is very nice.
3 I want a pen friend from England. I want .... to be a boy.
4 She is very friendly. One day I visited .... and .... went to the cinema.
5 I want to have a pen friend in another country. I prefer that he or .... comes from Holland.
6 I have many books that I don't need any more. I'd like to sell ....
7 I'm selling my computer because I've got no space for .... in my bedroom.

2 Work in pairs. Look at the picture of Hasan's bedroom. What does he like doing in his free time? Remember to use the correct pronouns.

Hasan has got a camera so I think he enjoys taking photographs with it.

3 Read Hasan's email in the exam task and check your ideas from Exercise 2.

✓ **Exam task**

For each question, write the correct answer. Write one word for each gap.

From: Hasan

My name (0) ....*is*........ Hasan Sadik but my friends call me Zan. I'm 13 and I live in Adana, Turkey. I (1) .... got two older sisters. (2) .... names are Ayla and Zeynep.

In my free time, I love listening (3) .... music. I also play the drums in the school band. I go to the cinema with my friends once (4) .... week. After the film, (5) .... sometimes have dinner in a pizza restaurant together. I usually have mushroom pizza – my favourite.

Please write soon and tell me (6) .... your family, friends and hobbies.

Best wishes

Hasan

3 Eating in, eating out

A

B

C

D

E

Grammar & Vocabulary

1 Match the texts (1–4) with the pictures (A–E). There is one extra picture.

● ● ●

This week we asked a group of teenagers:

Where do you have breakfast?

Here are some of their answers.

'There's never much time before school to sit down and have a big breakfast. I usually sit and have some biscuits before class on the steps outside school.' *Angela, 13*

(1) **C**

'In my house, we always have breakfast together in the kitchen. My mum usually puts some flowers from our garden on the table.' *Noelia, 12*

(2) ☐

'On the sofa in the living room, of course! If there aren't any cartoons on TV, I usually watch sports.' *Harun, 12*

(3) ☐

'Don't tell my mum but I sometimes have breakfast in my bedroom. I love hot chocolate. If there isn't any hot chocolate left, then I have some orange juice.' *Victor, 14*

(4) ☐

2 Work in pairs. Complete the table with these words (some items can go in more than one room).

bed	bookshelf	chair	cooker	cupboard
fridge	desk	lamp	mirror	shelf
	shower	sofa	toilet	

bedroom	bathroom	living room	kitchen
bed			

Grammar – *There is / are, a / an, some & any*

📝 » Page 93

3 Whose house is it? Write *Angela, Noelia, Harun* or *Victor.*

1 There's some hot chocolate on the desk in the bedroom. ....Victor....
2 There are some biscuits on the floor next to the stairs. ....
3 There aren't any cartoons on TV this morning so this person's watching sports. ....
4 There's a garden with some flowers. ....

4 👁 Exam candidates often make mistakes with *There is / are, a / an, some & any*. Correct one mistake in each of these sentences.

1 Can you bring with you ~~any~~ lemonade and crisps? ..some..
2 My mum works as a assistant chef.
3 In my room is there a sofa.
4 It's free so you don't need some money.
5 I bought some jeans and a beautiful trainers.
6 It's very small and there are a small bed and a desk.
7 It's an interesting place because there is a lot of different things to see.

Reading & Writing Part 4

1 Look at this text message conversation between Wendy and her grandma, and <u>underline</u> all of the verbs which talk about food.

> Grandma, I want to make a mushroom omelette. How do I make it?

> Break the eggs into a bowl, mix them with a little salt, and then cook them in butter. Cut up the mushrooms, and then add them to the eggs when the omelette is almost cooked.

> Thanks, Grandma!

2 Work in pairs. Discuss the meaning of the verbs in Exercise 1.

> I think 'add' means put with another thing.

> Yes, I agree.

💡 Exam tip

Read the text before and after the gap carefully, and think about what each option means before you choose one.

3 Look at this sentence, and the three options, A, B and C. Read the explanation below.

> Can you give me a .... to put this soup in?
>
> **A** knife **B** glass **C** bowl
>
> *A knife is used to cut something, a glass is something we drink water from, and we often have soup in a bowl, so C is the correct answer.*

4 Choose the correct option, A, B or C to complete these sentences.

1 That restaurant doesn't .... main courses, but you can get a snack and a drink there.
   A serve **B** eat **C** bring

2 When I look .... my little cousin, we often make cakes together.
   A for **B** after **C** at

3 Shall we ask the .... to bring us the menu?
   A chef **B** waiter **C** customer

4 When you .... food, you cook it in water.
   A bake **B** roast **C** boil

✓ Exam task

For each question, choose the correct answer.

Where I live

Moussa is 13 years old and he lives on a small **(1)** .... in Mali, West Africa. There are only two rooms in his house; one for his parents and the other for Moussa and his little brother, Sekou. Moussa gets up early and looks **(2)** .... Sekou while their mother makes breakfast. The family has breakfast together. They usually have bread with milk and **(3)** .... a little sugar to it. Moussa walks to school with his friends. It **(4)** .... them about ten minutes. When they get to school, they have to clean the classroom. At noon, Moussa goes home for lunch. For lunch the family often has vegetables which they have **(5)** .... themselves. When lunch is finished, Moussa **(6)** .... to school for afternoon lessons, and then goes home again for dinner in the evening.

	A		B		C
1	forest		farm		village
2	after		up		around
3	include		join		add
4	takes		needs		keeps
5	brought		grown		left
6	enters		arrives		returns

Grammar & Vocabulary

1 Complete the descriptions with words from the box. You don't need all the words.

> bread   burger   cheese   chicken   egg   fish
> jam   juice   meat   milk   omelette   onions
> ~~potatoes~~   rice   salad   soup   vegetables

2 Now match the descriptions (1–3) with the pictures (A–C).

1 I love *köttbullar*. These are Swedish meatballs. In our house we usually eat them with **(1)** ...potatoes... and a little bit of jam. We have a glass of **(2)** .... with it.
Picture: ....B....

2 I'm from Goa in India. We live next to the sea and we eat a lot of **(3)** .... with **(4)** ....
and vegetables. My mum cooks *kalputi* once a week – it's great. She fries fish with onions.
Picture: ....

3 I'm from Colombia and my favourite food is *ajiaco*. It's a kind of **(5)** ....
with **(6)** ...., potatoes and corn. I often drink **(7)** .... with it.
Picture: ....

Grammar – (*don't*) *have to*

▶▶ Page 93

3 Read the interview and answer the questions.

1 What is Josh's favourite food?
2 Where does he usually have lunch?

THIS WEEK WE MEET JOSH. HE'S FROM MELBOURNE, AUSTRALIA.

What's your favourite food?

I love fast food like burgers and pizza but I also like salad and vegetables.

Where do you usually have lunch?

We all have to stay at school for lunch. There isn't a school canteen (a kind of restaurant) so I buy my lunch from the tuck shop. That's a kind of school café. I have to pay for my lunch before school starts. At lunchtime, two students have to collect our food from the tuck shop and we eat it in the classroom. We don't have to wash up because we use paper plates and plastic forks.

Who cooks in your house?
Do you have to help?

Both my mum and my dad. No, I don't have to help.

A

B

C

4 Are these sentences true (T) or false (F)?

1 Josh can have his lunch at home on a school day. ....F....
2 Josh pays for his lunch before he eats it. ....
3 The people in the tuck shop take the food to the classrooms. ....
4 Josh often washes up the plates at school. ....

5 Josh's friend Susanna lives in Costa Rica in Central America. Complete their phone conversation with the correct form of (*don't*) *have to* and the verbs in brackets.

Josh: Hi, Susanna! How was school today?

Susanna: Terrible! My school day is very long and then we **(1)** ......have to do...... (do) a lot of homework.

Josh: Oh, really! **(2)** .... you .... (wake up) very early?

Susanna: Yes, I do. I **(3)** .... (get up) at 6.30 a.m. because the school bus leaves at seven o'clock.

Josh: **(4)** .... you .... (tidy) your room before school?

Susanna: No, I **(5)** .... (tidy) my room but I **(6)** .... (make) my bed. My brother **(7)** .... (make) the breakfast but I often don't have time to eat it at home so I **(8)** .... (eat) it on the bus.

Listening Part 2

1 🔊 09 Listen to a conversation in a fast food café and complete the menu with the prices.

Menu

A cheese omelette **(2)** £ ....

A fried egg **(1)** £ ....1.75...........

Hot drinks **(3)** .... p

Bread and butter **(4)** £ ....

A piece of cake **(5)** £ ....

2 Work in pairs. Read the notice and write questions to find out more information about the school trip.

What can we do there? How much is the trip?

3 Read the exam task. Which of your questions in Exercise 2 do you think the recording will answer?

School trip

School of Cooking

16th February

✓ Exam task

🔊 10 You will hear a teacher telling students about a school trip. For each question, write the correct answer in the gap. Write one word or a number or a date or a time.

School trip	
Date:	16th February
Name of school of cooking:	**(1)** ....
How we'll get there:	by **(2)** ....
Time to meet:	**(3)** .... a.m.
What we'll make:	**(4)** ....
Total price:	**(5)** £ ....

4 Work in pairs. Discuss these questions.

1 What's your favourite food?
2 Where do you usually have lunch?
3 Who cooks in your house? Do you have to help?

Speaking

Speaking Part 2
💬 ≫ Page 120

1 Match each reason (a–f) with what people like or don't like (1–6).

1   I like strawberries because
2   I don't like fast food because
3   I never eat in my school canteen because
4   I love breakfast because
5   I like going to restaurants because
6   I enjoy cooking because

a   the food there isn't very good.
b   I'm always hungry when I wake up!
c   it's fun to learn new things.
d   I can try new kinds of food.
e   it's not good for your health.
f   they're fresh and sweet.

> **Exam tip**
>
> In the first part of Part 2, you have to say if you like the things that you can see in pictures. Remember to give reasons for your answers.

2 🔊 11 Listen to six short conversations about food. Check your answers to Exercise 1.

3 🔊 12 Look at these pictures. Listen to two exam candidates talking about them. Which candidate gives the best answer? Why?

4 Work in pairs. Talk about the pictures in Exercise 3. Start your questions with 'Do you like … ?' and remember to give reasons for your answers.

✓ Exam task

Now, in this part of the test you are going to talk together. Here are some pictures that show different types of meals.

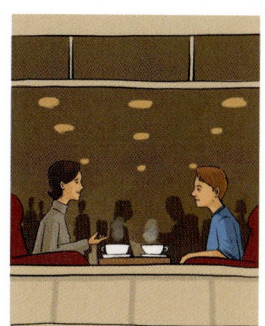

Do you like these different types of meals? Say why or why not.

Reading & Writing Part 7
✎ » Page 114

1 Look at the picture of students in a school canteen. Draw lines to match these phrases to the correct people. You can use the people more than once.

sitting at a table   walking to a table   serving the food

carrying lunch   taking a picture of lunch with a phone

eating lunch   chatting with friends   waiting to be served

2 Look at the verbs in Exercise 1 again. Can you put them into the past tense? Make sentences about the picture, then check your answers with a partner.

The girl carried her lunch to a table.

✓ **Exam task**

Look at the three pictures. Write the story shown in the pictures. Write 35 words or more.

3 ⊙ Exam candidates often make mistakes with the spelling of verbs in the past. Correct one mistake in each sentence.

1 After that it stoped raining and it was sunny.
2 At the party we danced and singed. It was very nice.
3 I went to a shopping centre to buy a new skirt and I payed 45 pounds for it.
4 I swam, went shopping and visitted my aunt.

4 Look at these two pictures, which tell a story. Work with a partner. Write three sentences about what happened in the story.

You could start like this: *A boy is in the kitchen ...*

💡 **Exam tip**

You have to write a story about what you see in the pictures. You can use present or past tenses to tell the story, but don't mix them: use past OR present for the whole story. Remember to spell the verbs correctly.

5 Check your story. Is your spelling correct? Have you mixed past and present? Now read your partner's story. Can you see any mistakes?

4 What are you doing now?

READERS' TIPS

Tips of the week!

Great places to do all your favourite sports.
Send us a tip and win some new sports clothes!

1 There's a new park behind the shopping centre that nobody uses. It's cool for BMX bikes too! On your way home, get some hot chocolate from Jack's Café! *Morgan, 14*

2 My granddad and I always go to Harts River. We don't catch very much there but we always have a good time. *Freddy, 15*

3 There are two new tables at the sports centre. Ask the receptionist for bats and balls. *Lucie, 13*

4 They're looking for new players at the ice rink. You have to be good at ice-skating, like fast ball sports and be fit. *Mel, 13*

5 You can practise throwing balls at Mike's Sports Shop on Saturday. Players from the city team will be there to give lessons. *Yolanda, 12*

6 The outdoor pool is open again! Go there after 6 p.m. and it's empty. *Neil, 11*

Grammar & Vocabulary

1 Work in pairs. Match the Readers' Tips above with these sports.

skateboarding `1`   table tennis ☐
swimming ☐   fishing ☐
ice hockey ☐   basketball ☐

2 Complete the table with these sports and those from Exercise 1. Then add more words to the table.

aerobics   athletics   cycling   football   golf
ice-skating   martial arts
skiing   surfing   volleyball

play	go	do
volleyball		

Grammar – Present continuous

» Page 94

3 Read the text. What sport are Nicolas and Sara playing at the moment?

Nicolas **is carrying** a racket and three small yellow balls. Now he**'s hitting** one of the balls with his racket. But what is Sara **doing**? She **isn't hitting** the ball, she **isn't playing** well today. Nicolas **is winning** 40–15 right now.

4 Exam candidates often make mistakes with the spelling of verbs in the present continuous. Correct five more mistakes in this message.

I'm bored. I'm ~~wrinting~~ *writing* this message outside school because I'm wating for my friends. Some of them are styding in the library and others are workin in class. What are you doing? Are you lisening to music? Oh – I can see my friends cooming now so I've got to go.

5 Complete Dan and Lucy's conversation with the correct form of the present continuous.

Dan: What **(1)** *are you doing* (you / do), Lucy?
Lucy: I **(2)** .... (watch) the basketball final with Freya.
Dan: **(3)** .... (the school team / win)?
Lucy: Yes, it **(4)** .... Harjeev **(5)** .... (play) really well.
Dan: **(6)** .... (Toby / sit) with you?
Lucy: No, he **(7)** .... He **(8)** .... (buy) some water at the café. Why?
Dan: I'm at his cousins' match. They **(9)** .... (lose).
Lucy: Oh, no! I'll tell him.

Listening Part 1

1 Work in pairs. Look at the exam questions in Exercise 2 and the exam task. Then complete these sentences with the correct number.

1 There are .... short conversations in this part.
2 You have to answer .... question(s) about each conversation.
3 Each question has got .... pictures. You have to choose the correct one.

💡 Exam tip

You will hear information about all three pictures but only one of the pictures answers the question correctly.

2 Read question 1 from the exam task below and look at the pictures. Then answer the questions.

1 What are the important words in this question? Underline them.
2 What is Cara doing in the three pictures?
   A ....
   B ....
   C ....

1 What's Cara doing now?

A   B   C

3 🔊 13 Listen and answer exam task question 1.

4 🔊 13 Listen again and match these questions with the pictures (A, B or C) from exam task question 1 above.

1 What's Cara doing now?
2 What did Cara miss today?
3 What does the boy think Cara is doing now?

✓ Exam task

🔊 14 For each question, choose the correct picture.

2 How much was Jenny's new tennis racket?

£35   £40   £45
A   B   C

3 What time does the hockey match start?

4:10   4:20   4:30
A   B   C

4 What is the boy drinking?

A   B   C

5 Who is the girl's table tennis coach?

A   B   C

Grammar & Vocabulary

1 Work in pairs. What sports do the people in the photos do?

2 Describe what the people are wearing. Use words from the box or your own ideas. Then describe what you and your friends are wearing.

> boots   coat   dress   helmet   jacket   jeans
> shirt   shoes   shorts   skirt   socks   sweater
> swimming costume   trainers   trousers   T-shirt

Grammar – Present continuous vs present simple

📝 ≫ Page 94

3 Match the texts (a–c) with the photos (1–3) in Exercise 1.

a Paula De Souza
Paula plays football for her local team. She trains for eight to ten hours a week and then she has to find time to do her homework. Right now, she's getting ready for a competition against a national under-16 team.

b Molly Singer
Molly is a swimmer. She swims every morning before she goes to school and she often swims in the evening, too. She's feeling excited because she's got a big race soon and she hopes to win a medal.

c Erol Badem
Erol comes from Turkey. He loves wheelchair basketball – his friends say he's the best player in their team. He's preparing for their next competition because he wants to win!

4 <u>Underline</u> examples of the present continuous and ⃝circle examples of the present simple in the texts in Exercise 3.

5 Complete the sentences with *present continuous* or *present simple*.

1 We use the .... to talk about the things we do regularly and with verbs that describe states, e.g. *like, hope* and *want*.

2 We use the .... to talk about things which are happening now.

6 Complete the text with the present continuous or the present simple of these verbs.

> ~~come~~   get   play   think   train   want

Teenager Joey Carter **(1)** ..comes.. from Detroit in the USA. He **(2)** .... baseball. In the winter he usually **(3)** .... very hard with his team. At the moment, Joey and the team **(4)** .... about the next big competition and Joey **(5)** .... ready. He **(6)** .... to win there but his dream is to play for a professional baseball team when he's older.

Reading & Writing Part 1

1 Work in pairs. Look at the exam task and answer these questions.

1   What type of texts are there?
2   How many possible answers are given for each text?

2 Look at this message. Work in pairs. Why did Ethan write the message to Richard? Choose A or B, and <u>underline</u> the part of the message that helped you to decide.

> Richard, is your bike OK now? Did the man at the bike shop repair it? I'm going cycling on Saturday. Are you interested? Ethan

A   Ethan is inviting Richard to go cycling with him.
B   Ethan is giving Richard advice about repairing his bike.

3 Look at these notices and messages and answer the questions. <u>Underline</u> the part of the text that tells you the answer.

1   Who should you ask if you want to know more about what this notice says?

> **Sports hall closed this week.**
> **For more information, speak to a member of staff.**

2   Which part of the message shows you that Ned is offering to help?

> Kim – Fabio said you need another player for the match on Friday. Is that right? I'm free, and I can be there by 2 p.m. Ned

3   Which part of the notice tells you that the special price is only for a short time?

> **Sports shop: Trainers now only £15.**
> **All must go. Hurry! Sale ends tomorrow.**

4 Look at the notices and messages in the exam task. Write if each one is a *message* or a *notice* and where you might see it.

✅ **Exam task**

For each question, choose the correct answer.

1
> Hi, Sandra. Are you going to hockey practice this evening? My brother's taking me, on his way to cricket. Shall we pick you up? Stefanie

A   Stefanie is offering Sandra a lift to hockey practice.
B   Stefanie is trying to find out if there is hockey practice today.
C   Stefanie is asking Sandra if she wants to do cricket instead of hockey.

2
> **The pool temperature is lower this week, as we are repairing the heating.**

A   The problem with the pool heating is now fixed.
B   The swimming pool is not open this week.
C   The water will not be as warm as usual.

3
> Dad, Sam called to ask me to play tennis. I've borrowed your racket – I don't know where mine is. Can you look for it? Katia

A   Katia wants her dad to play tennis with her.
B   Katia wants her dad to find her tennis racket.
C   Katia wants her dad to lend her his tennis racket.

4
> **Sale starts next Monday.**
> Large discounts on sports clothes, including 50% off all swimming costumes.

A   You will spend less if you buy sports clothes now.
B   Some sports clothes will be half the usual price.
C   Sports clothes in larger sizes will be cheaper.

5
> Football team: as the weather is good, come to the sports field for practice, this evening only. 8 p.m. as usual. Don't forget your kit!

A   The team should go to a different place today.
B   The practice will be at a different time today.
C   The team have to wear a different kit today.

Reading & Writing

✏️ >> Page 112

1 Look at the exam task below and answer the questions.

Write an email to Alice and answer the questions. Write 25 words or more.

1 What type of text do you need to write? Who to?
2 How many questions do you need to answer? What are they?
3 How many words do you have to write?

Read this email from your English friend, Alice.

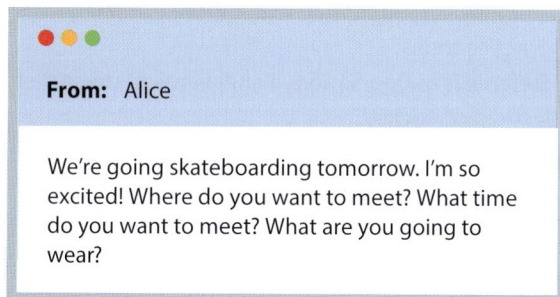

🔴🟠🟢

From: Alice

We're going skateboarding tomorrow. I'm so excited! Where do you want to meet? What time do you want to meet? What are you going to wear?

---

2 Work in pairs. Read these students' answers to the exam task in Exercise 1. Then decide together on the best answer and say why.

1 Dear Alice, I'm going to wear a T-shirt and shorts. Would you like to meet at midday, do you have a skateboard? I'm bringing mine.
Jason

2 Hi Alice,
I love skateboarding. Let's meet at the park. Shall we meet at 2 pm? I'm going to wear a jumper and jeans. See you,
Daniela

3 Let's meet at your house. Let's meet after lunch. I'm wearing a shirt and trousers.

3 Match the teacher's comments (a–c) with answers 1–3 in Exercise 2.

a You answer the three questions but you should start with Dear or Hi and the person's name and end with your name. The answer is also too short.

b This is an email and you use 25 words or more but you don't answer all the questions. Also, you make mistakes with punctuation, capital letters and full stops.

c Well done! You write a clear email, you use 25 words or more and you answer all three questions very well.

💡 **Exam tip**

Remember to answer all three questions or you will lose marks.

✓ **Exam task**

Read the email from your English friend, Ed.

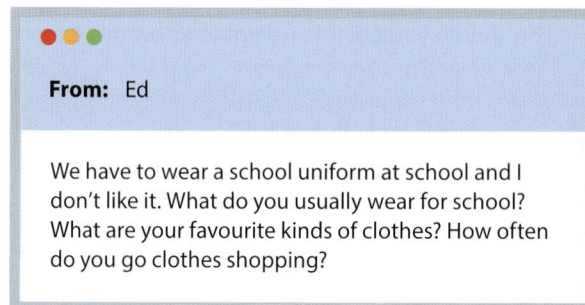

🔴🟠🟢

From: Ed

We have to wear a school uniform at school and I don't like it. What do you usually wear for school? What are your favourite kinds of clothes? How often do you go clothes shopping?

Write an email to Ed and answer the questions. Write 25 words or more.

4 Work in small groups. Read each other's exam task answers. Can you answer 'yes' to these questions? If so, it is probably a good answer.

1 Is it an email?
2 Does it answer all three questions?
3 Are there 25 words or more?

Speaking Part 2
>> Page 120

A

B

C

1 Work in pairs. Look at the pictures. Say what the people are wearing.

2 Match these questions (1–3) with the pictures (A–C).

1 Are you interested in fashion? Why? / Why not?
2 Do you spend a lot of time deciding what to wear? Why? / Why not?
3 Do you prefer wearing sports clothes or jeans? Why?

3 🔊 **15** Listen to two exam candidates answering the questions in Exercise 2.
Who gives the best answers, the boy or the girl? Why?

4 Complete these sentences with an adjective from the box.

> brighter   cheaper   comfortable
> fun   prettier   warm

1 I like sports clothes more than jeans because they're more .... to wear.
2 I prefer wearing boots to shoes because they keep me .... in cold weather.
3 It's more .... buying clothes in a shop than online because you can try them on.
4 I buy clothes from the market because of the prices. They're .... than in the shops.
5 I'm going to buy the blue sweater because it's .... than the white one. The white one is quite boring.
6 I love the team's new kit. The colours are much ...., so everyone will see us!

5 Look at the questions in Exercise 2 again. Work in pairs to ask and answer the questions.

☑ Exam task

Take turns to be the examiner and the candidate.

The examiner reads the question and the candidate answers.

1 Who decides what clothes to buy – you, or your parents? Why?
2 Do you borrow clothes from other people that you live with? Why? / Why not?
3 Do you wear different clothes when you're not at school? Why? / Why not?

💡 Exam tip

If the examiner asks you about what you prefer, remember to give reasons for your answer.

5 Great places to visit

PLACES & BUILDINGS

1 I'm waiting to buy a ticket at the ....cinema...... I want to see the new *Star Wars* film.

2 Mum's showing me the Ancient Egypt room. We're in the ....

3 My grandma wants to buy a new hat and a pair of shoes. She's shopping in the ....

4 I'm having an ice cream at the .... The second part of the play is starting soon.

5 My dad's talking to a police officer in the .... because he's lost his wallet.

6 It's my cousin's birthday. We're looking for a book about tennis for her in the ....

7 I'm visiting my brother. He's studying science at the ....

8 My mum is buying medicine at the ....

Grammar & Vocabulary

1 Where are the people above? Complete the sentences with these words.

> bookshop cinema department store
> museum pharmacy police station
> theatre university

Grammar – Past simple positive

>> Page 95

2 Read the text. Where is Javier?

Hi, guys! I'm in a capital city in Europe. We got here two days ago. In the morning we explored the castle. Then we had lunch on Princes Street, which is a busy shopping street. My sister stopped at a clothes shop and I was really bored. Then we went to the National Museum of Scotland. I enjoyed the Ancient Egypt room because we studied that in history.

3 Underline the regular past simple verbs and circle the irregular past simple verbs in the text in Exercise 2.

4 Exam candidates often make mistakes with past simple verbs. Correct one mistake in each of these sentences.

1 I enjoed my party very much. All my friends were there.
2 My new mobile phone costed £150.
3 We traveled to Niagara Falls and I met my cousin there.
4 I think I lefted my school bag at your house last night.

5 Complete the text with the past simple positive form of the verbs in brackets.

Levi Strauss (1) .... (be) born on 26th February 1829 in Germany. When his father (2) .... (die), Levi Strauss (3) .... (move) to New York to join his brothers. In 1848, people (4) .... (find) gold in California and there (5) .... (be) a lot of money there. Levi Strauss (6) .... (decide) to move to San Francisco, California and he (7) .... (begin) to sell things like shirts, trousers and umbrellas. In 1872, one of his customers (8) .... (write) him a letter. Men (9) .... (need) strong trousers to wear at work. The customer, Jacob Davis, (10) .... (try) putting small pieces of metal on the trousers and the first jeans (11) .... (be) born. The two men (12) .... (open) their jeans factory in San Francisco and the rest is history!

Reading & Writing Part 2

Grammar – Past simple negative

📝 » **Page 95**

1 Look at the sentences and answer the questions.

Levi Strauss wasn't born in the USA. He was born in Germany.

They didn't build their factory in New York. They built it in San Francisco.

1 What's the past simple negative form of *be*?

2 How do we make the past simple negative form of most other verbs?

2 Read the questions in the exam task. Can you find a verb in the past simple negative?

> 💡 **Exam tip**
>
> Read the questions in Part 2 carefully. If you see a negative verb, remember that the information in the text may be positive.

3 Complete these questions about some school trips with the past simple negative form of the verb in brackets.

1 Who .... (enjoy) the school trip to the museum?

2 Who .... (have) to wake up early for the school trip?

3 Who .... (go) on the school trip?

4 Who .... (see) the famous painting in the museum?

5 Who .... (arrive) on time to get on the coach?

6 Who .... (be) happy about travelling by train?

4 Look at the questions in Exercise 3 again. Which questions are asking about someone's opinion?

5 Read the texts about a school trip. Who enjoyed the trip?

Freddie

> We went to an art museum. I've never really looked at paintings before. A guide explained some of the most famous ones to us. I thought it was really interesting.

Lucas

> Usually, school trips are really fun. This one wasn't. We went to the zoo. It was too hot, and all the animals were sleeping.

✅ **Exam task**

For each question, choose the correct answer.

		Ella	Carole	Tina
1	Who is happy with the photos she took at the castle?	A	B	C
2	Who found out something which surprised her?	A	B	C
3	Who wants to return to the castle?	A	B	C
4	Who didn't like the school work she had to do?	A	B	C
5	Who preferred seeing the outside of the castle to the inside?	A	B	C

My trip to the castle

Ella

We had a picnic outside in the castle garden, and then we went on a tour of the inside. That was my favourite part of the day. We had to do some schoolwork too, of course! We wrote down information and took photos for a project. We didn't really have enough time at the castle, so I think I'll ask my parents to take me again.

Carole

The teacher asked us to sit in the garden of the castle and draw a picture of it when we arrived. My friends all said that was really boring, and I agreed. After that we had a tour of the inside. I didn't think anyone lived in castles any more, but there's still a family living in this one. That's amazing!

Tina

Before our visit we wrote down some questions about the castle, and had to find the answers while we were there. It made the day more interesting. We walked around some of the rooms in the castle, but I had more fun in the garden, taking pictures with my new camera. They look really brilliant on my bedroom wall.

Win a trip to your favourite capital city! Just answer these questions.

1 When were the Olympics first in London?
- **A** 1908
- **B** 1948
- **C** 2012

2 When did Apple sell its first iPad?
- **A** April 2009
- **B** April 2010
- **C** April 2011

3 When did the first online bookshop start selling books?
- **A** 1995
- **B** 2000
- **C** 2005

4 When did the first cinema open?
- **A** March 21st, 1909
- **B** March 21st, 1899
- **C** March 21st, 1809

5 When did customers in a department store first take the lift?
- **A** Tuesday 23rd March, 1937
- **B** Wednesday 23rd March, 1887
- **C** Monday 23rd March, 1857

Email your answers to rita@winatrip.com. Don't forget to say where you'd like to go!

1 Work in pairs. Answer the competition questions.

2 Check your answers on page 140. Which pair(s) of students have got the most correct answers?

3 Work in pairs. Take turns to say these dates.

> March 31st   Wednesday 5th
> 20th August, 2007   July 1998
> Tuesday 3rd February, 2019

Grammar – Past simple questions

📝 » Page 95

4 Look at the questions in the competition and answer these questions.

1 How do we form past simple questions with *be*? (look at question 1)
2 How do we form past simple questions with most other verbs? (look at questions 2–5)

5 👁 Exam candidates often make mistakes with past simple questions. Correct one mistake in each question.

1 What presents ~~do you get~~ on your last birthday?
   did you get
2 Did you enjoyed your holiday?
3 Why you not come to the party?
4 What have you done on your holiday?
5 How you know I bought a mobile phone?

Grammar – *ago & past simple*

📝 » Page 95

6 Complete these sentences with a number. What word do we use to tell us when something happened?

1 Customers first used a lift in a department store almost .... centuries ago.
2 The first online bookshop started selling books nearly .... years ago.
3 Apple sold its first iPad almost .... months ago.
4 The Olympics were first in London .... years ago.
5 The first cinema opened more than .... years ago.

7 Write six sentences about when you did these things.

> visit a museum
> go shopping in a department store
> play sport in a sports centre
> see a film at the cinema
> buy something in an online shop
> borrow a book from the library

I visited a museum with my family three weeks ago.

Listening Part 2

1 Work in pairs. Look at these places from the exam task and answer the questions.

> Dolby Theater   Lucky Devils   Staples Center
> Chinese Theater   Hollywood Boulevard

1 What part of the world is the exam task about?
2 The Chinese Theater is a cinema. What are the other places? If you don't know, guess.

2 Look at the exam task. What kinds of words do you think you will hear in each space?

Date: 5th March, 17th June, etc.

3 🔊 16 Listen to Selena talking about her trip to Hollywood, California, and complete the answers.

1 When was Selena's birthday?
.... April
2 When did Selena arrive in Los Angeles?
.... morning
3 What day did Selena go to Staples Center?
....
4 When did Selena return?
.... days ago

💡 Exam tip

You often have to complete information about a price. Make sure you write the correct price.

☑ Exam task

🔊 17 For each question, write the correct answer in each gap. Write one word or a number or a date or a time.

You will hear some information about a tour for young people.

Hollywood tour for young people	
Name of tour:	Hollywood Living
Date:	(1) ....
Place to meet:	at (2) .... Hollywood Boulevard
Type of food for lunch:	(3) ....
Stadium tour includes:	a (4) .... game
Cost for children:	(5) $ ....

4 Work in pairs. Find some information about a place (or places) in your town. Then write three competition questions. Use the questions in the competition on page 32 to help you.

1 Where was the library before 2008?
A near the museum
B near the police station
C near the bank

5 Work in small groups. Ask and answer your competition questions.

> 1 Where was the library before 2008? – A, near the museum; B, near the police station or C, near the bank?

> Was it near the bank?

> Yes, it was.

Reading & Writing

1 Work in pairs. Julieta and her family went shopping last Saturday. Look at the picture and talk together about the different places they went to.

2 Work in pairs. You receive this email from a friend. How do you think Berta is feeling?

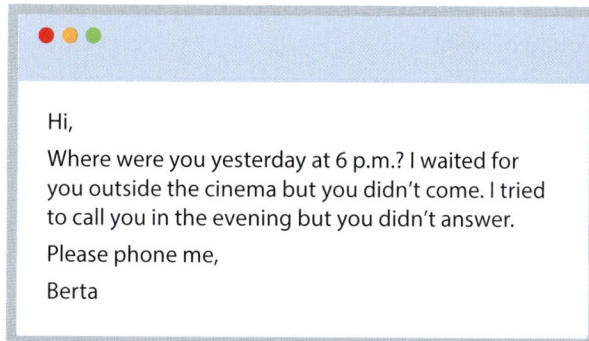

> Hi,
>
> Where were you yesterday at 6 p.m.? I waited for you outside the cinema but you didn't come. I tried to call you in the evening but you didn't answer.
>
> Please phone me,
> Berta

3 Read these two answers to Berta's email. Which one is better? Why?

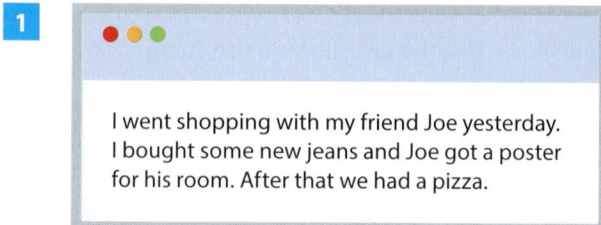

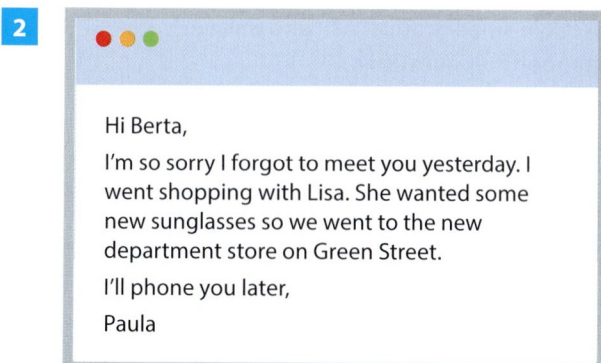

1
> I went shopping with my friend Joe yesterday. I bought some new jeans and Joe got a poster for his room. After that we had a pizza.

2
> Hi Berta,
>
> I'm so sorry I forgot to meet you yesterday. I went shopping with Lisa. She wanted some new sunglasses so we went to the new department store on Green Street.
>
> I'll phone you later,
> Paula

💡 **Exam tip**

If you start and finish your note, email or postcard well, you will do better in this part.

4 Complete the table with these expressions.

Best wishes   Bye for now
Dear John   Hello   Hi   See you soon

starting	finishing
Hi	Best wishes

Now do the exam task.

✓ **Exam task**

Yesterday, you went shopping in your town. Write an email to your English friend, Zoe.

Say:

- **who** you went with
- **what** you bought
- **what** you did after shopping.

Write **25 words** or more.

5 Read your exam task email again. If you can answer 'yes' to these questions, it is probably a good answer.

1 Do you open and close your email with expressions like *Hi!* and *Bye for now*?
2 Do you include all three pieces of information?
3 Do you use some of the words and expressions from the unit?
4 Is your email 25 words or more?

MY FAMILY'S YEAR IN ASIA

10TH APRIL

Last weekend we went to Singapore and had a brilliant time. On Saturday morning, we visited the Science Centre, which is a science museum, and then in the afternoon we went shopping on Orchard Road, the main shopping street. I bought some clothes from TANGS, a department store, and my dad got a new camera, which takes great photos. After a very long day, we were all in bed at 9.00 pm. On Sunday, we explored the Bird Park in the morning. We saw a lot of different types of parrots. Another amazing weekend!

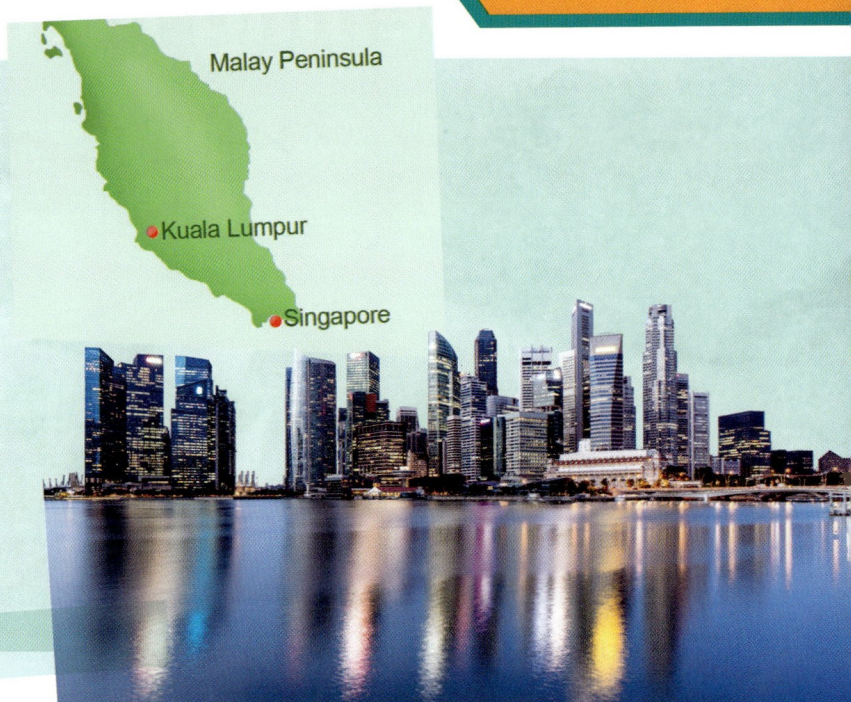

Malay Peninsula
Kuala Lumpur
Singapore

Speaking Part 1

💬 ≫ Page 119

Grammar – Time expressions: *in/at/on*

📋 ≫ Page 96

1 Work in pairs. Read Bettina's blog above and answer these questions.

1 Where did she go last weekend?
2 What did she do?

2 Look at Bettina's blog again and complete the rules with *in*, *at* or *on*.

1 We use .... with days of the week and special days (e.g. *my birthday*).
2 We use .... with parts of the day (e.g. *the morning, the afternoon*, etc.), months and years.
3 We use .... with times, the weekend and night.
4 We do not use *in*, *at* or .... before *last* or *next* (e.g. *last weekend*).

3 Write questions about the things your partner did this week. Use the table to help you or use your own ideas.

What		do	at / in / on	6.30 p.m. yesterday?
Where	did you	eat		the evening?
When		go		Tuesday?

What did you do in the evening?

4 🔊 **18** Listen to two exam candidates answering the same questions. Do they both answer the questions well? Why? / Why not?

💡 Exam tip

You will sometimes get a question about the past in the exam. Remember to answer questions about *yesterday*, *last night*, etc. with the past simple. If you say when you did the activity, use *in*, *at* or *on* correctly.

5 Work in pairs. Read the examiner's questions and improve the boy's answers.

Examiner: What did you do yesterday after school?
Boy: (Go library, do homework.)
(1) *I went to the library at five o'clock and I did my homework.*

Examiner: What did you have for dinner?
Boy: (Pasta.) **(2)** ....
Examiner: What time did you go to bed?
Boy: (Ten o'clock.) **(3)** ....
Examiner: Thank you.

✓ Exam task

Student A, you are the examiner. Ask three of your questions from Exercise 3.

Student B, you are the candidate. Answer A's questions. Remember to use the past simple and to use *in*, *at* or *on* correctly.

Grammar & Vocabulary

1 Work in pairs. Complete the table with the types of transport you can see in the picture. Can you add any more words?

sea	land	air
ship		

2 Complete the timeline with the verbs in the box.

cycle   ~~drive~~   fly   ride   sail   walk

History timeline: Transport

1910	Many people began to **(1)** ......*drive*...... cars.
1932	Amelia Earhart became the first woman to **(2)** .... alone across the Atlantic Ocean.
1969	Neil Armstrong was the first person to **(3)** .... on the moon.
1970s	People started to **(4)** .... modern mountain bikes.
2010	16-year-old Jessica Watson was the youngest person to **(5)** .... around the world, in her pink boat.
2015	London teenager Tom Davies was the youngest person to **(6)** .... around the world on his bike.

Grammar – Comparative adjectives

📝 » Page 97

3 Work in pairs. Complete the transport facts with the adjectives in brackets.

1 In 2018, the airport in Atlanta, USA is .... (busy) than the airport in Shanghai, China.
2 The Airbus 380 passenger plane was .... (big) than the Boeing 777.
3 Australia is .... (far) from the USA than Italy.
4 A Rolls Royce is a .... (expensive) car than a Fiat.
5 A petrol car is .... (noisy) than an electric car.
6 The Chinese Bullet Train is .... (fast) than the French TGV.

4 👁 Exam candidates often make mistakes with comparative adjectives. Correct one mistake in each sentence.

1 The sweater was expensive. It cost £140. The shoes were ~~cheapper~~. ...*cheaper*....
2 My room is biger than my parents'. ....
3 My yunnger brother bought me a watch for my birthday. ....
4 We're going to go to the sports centre by car because that's more safer. ....
5 I bought the more new mobile phone because it has a camera. ....

5 Complete the text with the comparative form of the adjectives in brackets.

I never take the bus because buses are **(1)** .....*slower*...... (slow) than any other type of transport in my town. Even walking is **(2)** .... (fast) than taking the bus! I love travelling by train but the train is **(3)** .... (expensive) than the bus. We've got a new train station in our town. It's **(4)** .... (big) than the bus station and it's **(5)** .... (modern) than our airport. I often ride my bike because it's **(6)** .... (cheap) and **(7)** .... (healthy), too.

A [..................]

B [..................]

C [..................]

Listening Part 5

1 Look at the pictures. Yolanda met her friends at the cinema yesterday. Ask and answer questions about how they got there.

> How did A get to the cinema?

> She went by bike, she didn't go on foot.

💡 Exam tip

For each person (1–5), you often hear two of the words (A–H) but only one of them is correct. The answer can be the first or second word you hear.

2 🔊 19 Listen to Yolanda talking to her mum about her friends. How did they get to the cinema? Choose the correct answer.

1 Kathy
  A went by bus.
  B went on foot.

2 Lisa
  A walked.
  B borrowed her brother's bike.

3 Sofia
  A took the bus.
  B cycled.

3 Look at your answers to Exercise 2 and write the correct names (Kathy, Lisa or Sofia) in the spaces (A–C) in Exercise 1.

✓ Exam task

🔊 20 For each question, choose the correct answer.

You will hear Ethan and his mum talking about his birthday party. How will each person travel to the party?

People		Transport
0 Sister	B	**A** bike
1 Grandma	☐	**B** bus
2 Granddad	☐	**C** car
3 Uncle Tom	☐	**D** motorbike
4 Cousin Ursula	☐	**E** taxi
5 Aunt May	☐	**F** tram
		G train
		H underground

4 Work in pairs. Ask and answer questions about how you go to different places and say why. Use the words and phrases from the box or your own ideas.

> the town centre   school   sports practice
> your friend's house

> How do you go to school?

> I usually go on foot but when I'm late, I go by car because it's quicker.

1 Work in pairs. Read this short text. What does the underlined word mean? Choose the correct meaning, A, B or C. Which words in the text helped you choose the answer?

> The train was really <u>crowded</u>. There was someone sitting in every seat, and a lot of people standing up too.
>
> A full of people B late C comfortable to sit on

💡 Exam tip

Sometimes you will read a word which you don't understand. If you need to understand this word to answer one of the questions, use the text around the word to help you guess what it means.

2 Work in pairs. Read the text. Guess the meaning of the underlined words.

I went on a plane with my family last week. It was very exciting because it was my first time on a plane! My suitcase <u>weighed</u> a lot, because I put too much in it so it was difficult for me to carry. When we got to the airport, the staff told us there was a <u>delay</u>. We had to wait an extra hour, but finally we got on the plane. The <u>passenger</u> who was sitting next to me was really friendly. I was a little <u>frightened</u> about flying, but he told me that it's a really safe way to travel, so I felt better. The only bad thing was that my suitcase got <u>lost</u>. Everyone else collected their cases when we arrived, but mine wasn't there! I got it back two days later.

💡 Exam tip

There will sometimes be a question about why the text was written. To answer this type of question you need to look at the whole text.

3 Work in pairs. Read these short texts and decide why they were written. Choose A, B or C.

1 Our bikes are the best in town – come and see for yourself.
   A to check   B to sell   C to explain

2 If you have seen my bag, which is red and black, please call this number.
   A to thank   B to give advice   C to ask for help

3 It was so nice of you to give me a lift home from the party.
   A to offer help   B to thank   C to describe

4 Unfortunately, some trains will be late today because of the bad weather.
   A to explain   B to invite   C to agree

5 The buses in my town are green, with two floors and lots of big windows.
   A to describe   B to change   C to ask

6 You need the Northern Line. It's the black one on the London Underground map.
   A to give a reason   B to check   C to give information

4 Work in pairs. Follow the instructions and answer the questions about the exam task on page 39.

1 Look at the title and the picture in the exam task.
   a What do you think the text is about?
   b Why would someone write a text about this? Use one of the verbs from Exercise 3.

2 Sometimes words that you may not know are explained in the text. Read the words under the picture and question 4.
   a What does *invent* mean?
   b What does *inventions* mean ?

3 If you see a word from the text in an option, this doesn't always mean that option is correct. Read the second paragraph of the text and question 1.
   a Which sentence and which option in question 1 includes these words?

grandfather   competition   mother

   b Read this sentence from the end of the second paragraph.
   Alexis wanted to help.
   Did she want to help her grandfather or win a competition or help someone else with a problem? Which option in question 1 is correct, A, B or C?

☑ **Exam task**

For each question, choose the correct answer.

A new type of transport

Alexis Lewis is a teenager from the USA. She likes to invent – to think of new ideas for things that no one has made before, and then make them.

Alexis often enters competitions for young inventors. When she was younger she spent time with her grandfather, who made transport for people to go to space. One day Alexis' mother told her about a newspaper article which explained how difficult it was to get sick people through the countryside to hospital in Africa. Alexis wanted to help.

Alexis knew that in North America, before there were cars, horses pulled heavy things on a travois (a type of sledge), made of wood. Alexis thought people could do the same, but she added wheels. To make her travois light, she used bamboo, a plant which grows in Africa, not wood.

To pull Alexis' travois, you wear a belt, which means you can carry or hold other things. Alexis thinks her travois might be useful for carrying food home from the market, as well as taking people to hospital. Now it's finished, she's writing instructions for building one so people in Africa can make it themselves.

With help from US companies, Alexis plans to give ten travois free to hospitals in Africa. She doesn't want money for them because they are for poor people.

Alexis doesn't know if she wants to be an inventor when she's older, because she also likes music and writing, but she thinks it's important for children to learn about inventing at school.

1 Why did Alexis decide to invent a new type of transport?
   A She wanted to win a competition.
   B Her mother told her about a problem.
   C Her grandfather worked on spaceships.

2 How is Alexis' travois different from those pulled by horses?
   A It is heavier.
   B It is made of wood.
   C It has wheels.

3 What does the writer say about using Alexis' travois?
   A People will need instructions to use it.
   B People should not use it to carry shopping.
   C People can pull it without using their hands.

4 What does the writer say about Alexis' future?
   A She might do something different from inventing.
   B She would like to teach children how to invent.
   C She hopes she can start to sell her inventions.

5 What is the writer doing in this text?
   A advertising a new way to travel
   B telling the story of someone's idea
   C asking for help with a problem

Reading & Writing

Reading & Writing Part 5

Grammar – Superlative adjectives

📝 » Page 97

1 Look at the photo of a city street.
What do you think this is and where is it?

2 Read the text and check your ideas.

Shibuya is probably the most famous crossing in the world because it's also one of the busiest crossings in the world. When the traffic lights change, all the traffic stops and hundreds of people cross the road. On one of the most crowded corners of the Shibuya crossing is a statue of a famous dog called Hachikō. Many young people meet their friends here on a free afternoon.

3 Complete the facts with the superlative form of the adjectives in brackets.

- **(1)** ......The longest...... (long) bridge in the world is in China. It's a railway bridge and it's 165 km long. **(2)** .... (long) road bridge is in Thailand and it's over 50 km.
- **(3)** .... (big) roundabout in the world is probably in Malaysia. If you drive around the roundabout, you drive 3.5 km.
- As for traffic lights, **(4)** .... (old) traffic light is in the Small Town Museum in Ohio, USA.
- Los Angeles in the United States has got some of **(5)** .... (bad) traffic jams in the world. In 2017, drivers spent about 100 hours a year waiting in traffic there!

4 Complete the sentences with one word.

1 This is the .... amazing city in the world.
2 This bridge is shorter .... the bridge in my town.
3 They .... walking across the bridge right now.
4 My sister did .... find any clothes at the market.
5 You have .... turn right at the traffic lights.
6 There .... a lot of cars in town yesterday.

💡 **Exam tip**

Think of words that usually go together in certain sentences, e.g. *It's more crowded than the market.* or *It's the most famous crossing in the world.*

✓ **Exam task**

For each question, write the correct answer.

Write one word for each gap.

From: Zeynep

Hi Erol,

I'm in San Francisco **(0)** ......with...... my family right now and we **(1)** .... having an amazing time. The flight here was good. We went to the airport **(2)** .... taxi so my mum or dad didn't have **(3)** .... drive.
San Francisco is wonderful. I think it is the **(4)** .... beautiful city in the world. We took a tram to the top of a hill two days **(5)** .... We could see a lot of places from there. Then yesterday, we sailed under the Golden Gate Bridge. It is much bigger **(6)** .... the bridge in my city.
Write back soon!
Zeynep

Speaking Part 2

>> Page 120

1 Look at the pictures and choose an adjective to complete the examiner's questions.

amazing   boring   cheap   exciting
fun   interesting

Examiner
1 Do you think going to school by boat is ....?
2 Do you think going to school by train is ....?

2 🔊 21 Listen to Leyla answering the first question and check your ideas. Complete Leyla's answers.

Examiner: Do you think going to school by boat is exciting, Leyla?
Leyla: .... really.
Examiner: Why not?
Leyla: Because I sometimes feel .... on boats.

3 🔊 22 Now listen to the examiner asking Tomas and Leyla the second question and check your ideas in Exercise 1. What does the examiner say after Leyla's answer?

4 🔊 22 Listen to Tomas and Leyla answering the second question again.

1 Why doesn't Tomas think travelling to school by train is fun?
2 Why does Leyla like travelling by train?

💡 Exam tip

Remember, when you answer the examiner's questions, you need to give reasons for your answers.

5 Look at the underlined parts of these sentences. Work in pairs. Use the words from the box to say the same thing in a different way.

fast   free   traffic

1 I like trains because they are a quick way to travel.
they go very fast
2 I don't like driving because there are so many cars on the roads.
3 Bikes are a great way to travel because you don't have to buy a ticket!

6 🔊 23 When you've finished answering the examiner's questions, they will ask you a final question about the topic/subject shown in the pictures. Listen, and complete the examiner's question.

Examiner: Which of these ways of travelling to school do you ....
.... ?

✓ Exam task

Look again at the pictures that show different ways to travel.

Work in pairs. Answer these questions.

1 Do you think travelling by train is boring?
2 Do you think travelling by bike is dangerous?
3 Do you think travelling by boat is fun?
4 Do you think travelling by taxi is expensive?
5 Do you think travelling by car is comfortable?
6 Which of these ways of travelling do you like best? Why?

Grammar & Vocabulary

EDUCATION

1 Read the sentences and write the school subject.

1 So what's 345 and 67? It isn't 403, is it? m.aths...........

2 Now you have to draw a picture of something you like. a....................

3 Can you sing louder? I can't hear you. m....................

4 At the beginning of the 18th century, people moved to the towns. h....................

5 The past of *do* is *did* and the past participle is *done*. E....................

6 And of course H_2O is water and CO_2 is carbon dioxide. s....................

7 The Caspian Sea is the world's largest lake but it's also a sea. g....................

2 Choose the correct word to complete the questions.

1 What subject does your favourite teacher *learn / teach* you?

2 What do you have to do if you *lose / miss* a class?

3 How often do you worry before you *take / pass* an exam?

4 Did you *study / learn* how to swim at your school?

5 How much time do you *spend / use* doing your homework?

Grammar – *must / mustn't*

📝 » Page 98

3 Read these unusual school rules and answer the questions. Underline the word(s) which give you the answer.

> We must wear jackets and tights all year, even in the summer. Holly, 13 years old, UK.
>
> You mustn't walk or sit on the grass in winter because it's wet. Tina, 15 years old, Italy.

1 Can Holly take off her jacket when she's hot?

2 Can Tina and her friends have a picnic on the grass every day?

4 Complete the school rules with *must* or *mustn't* and the verbs in the box.

> be take use walk wear

1 Shh! You ..must be.. quiet in the library.

2 Put your phone in your bag, you know you .... your mobile phone in class.

3 No photos here. You .... photos anywhere in the school.

4 Where's your swimming cap? You know you .... it at the pool.

5 Keep left everyone! You ....on the left on the stairs.

Grammar – *should / shouldn't*

📝 » Page 98

5 Work in pairs. Look at the conversation and answer the questions.

Lars: You look worried. What's the matter?
Becky: I've got an exam tomorrow.
Lars: You should go to bed early and you shouldn't study all night.

1 Does Lars think it's a good idea to go to bed early before an exam?

2 Does Lars think it's a good idea to study all night before an exam?

6 Complete the sentences with *should* or *shouldn't* and the verbs in brackets.

1 You ..should read.. the instructions carefully and you ..should look.. at the example. (read ✓, look ✓)

2 You .... about the exam. You .... calm. (worry ✗, be ✓)

3 You .... all the questions even if you aren't sure about the answer. (answer ✓)

4 You .... your work before you finish. (check ✓)

5 You .... in pen on the answer sheet. You .... a pencil. (write ✗, use ✓)

Reading & Writing Part 1

1 Read notices 1–4 and underline the important words. Tick (✓) the sentence below (a or b) which means the same thing.

1 Please be quiet when you are in the library.

a You mustn't speak here. ✓
b You can speak quietly in the library. ☐

2 You should bring your teacher a note if you miss a class.

a You shouldn't miss class. ☐
b If you don't go to school, your parents should write to the school. ☐

3 Jamila – I asked the new maths teacher about our homework. You said she wants it on Friday, but actually she wants it tomorrow! Ayla

a Jamila must take her homework to school tomorrow. ☐
b Jamila must ask the teacher about her homework. ☐

4 No running inside the school building. Run in the playground only, please.

a You must walk at all times in the school. ☐
b Don't run in the school playground. ☐

2 Look at question 1 in the exam task below. Options A and C both have an expression which means the same as *return* in the notice, but which one also has a word which means the same as *correct*?

✓ Exam task

For each question, choose the correct answer.

1 Library. Please help staff by returning all books, films, etc. to the correct shelf.

A You need to give everything you have borrowed back to the library now.
B You must ask the staff if you are not sure where to find something.
C You should put things back in the right place when you finish.

2 Marta – Why weren't you at school today? Mrs Ross talked about the trip. I offered to take your letter, but she'll send it. Diana

A Marta must tell the teacher if she wants to go on the trip.
B Marta will get a letter about the trip in the post.
C Diana has got a letter for Marta about the trip.

3 SCHOOL SHOP. Don't miss our end of year sale. 50% discount on all books.

A Books are cheaper now.
B The sale is nearly finished.
C The shop is going to close.

4 ART CLUB starts at 4 p.m. on Monday. Try a different art activity each week until the end of term. Interested? Tell Mr Thomas before Friday.

The notice tells students

A what to do if they want to join the club.
B what type of art they will be doing at the club.
C what time the club finishes each week.

5 Lucia – I've just found your dictionary in my bag. I forgot to give it back to you after I borrowed it today. Sorry! Carlos

Carlos is telling Lucia that

A he forgot to lend her something.
B he has something which belongs to her.
C he has lost something which she gave him.

6 SCHOOL CONCERT. Friday at 8 p.m. Hurry – there are a few tickets left. £2 each.

The notice tells students that

A the tickets are cheaper now.
B they mustn't be late for the concert.
C tickets for the concert are still available.

Grammar & Vocabulary

1 Work in pairs. Look at the picture and talk about the musical instruments you can see.

2 Read the text about Camila Rodriguez. What does she teach?

> Camila Rodriguez comes from Bolivia, South America. When Camila was 11 she could play the violin well and her dream was to become a musician. Now she plays in three different orchestras and she's a teacher in her town's music school. Most of her students can't buy their own instruments because they don't have enough money but it doesn't matter. They can borrow their instruments from the school.

Grammar – can / could

📝 ≫ Page 99

3 Work in pairs. Look at the text in exercise 2 again and answer the questions. <u>Underline</u> where you found the answers in the text.

1 Did Camila learn to play an instrument when she was young?
2 Why do Camila's students borrow their instruments from the school?

4 Complete the email with *could* or *can* (✓) and *couldn't* or *can't* (✗) and the verb in brackets.

From: Tony

I've got some news! I'm in a band. Yes, I know I **(1)** ..*can't play*.. (✗ play) an instrument and I
(2) .... (✗ sing) but I **(3)** .... (✓ learn) to play the guitar. What about Adele, the British singer? She **(4)** .... (✓ sing) when she was four years old but she **(5)** .... (✗ play) the guitar until she was 17. Anyway, my friend Dave **(6)** .... (✓ write) well so he's writing the songs. My sister Lizzie **(7)** .... (✓ sing) so she's our singer. Would you like to join our band?

---

5 Work in pairs. Ask and answer questions about the musical instruments you and people you know can play.

Can you play an instrument?

Yes, I can. I can play the guitar.

Can you play an instrument?

No, I can't, but I'd like to play the piano.

Listening Part 2

Grammar – Adverbs of manner

📝 ≫ Page 100

1 Read this short text about a famous person. Who is it?

He was born in Italy in 1452 and he was good at a lot of different things; for example, he could draw and paint well and he could play music and sing beautifully. He probably didn't do anything badly! In the 15th century, only boys from the richest families went to school. Leonardo didn't go to school, but he learned to read, write and to do simple maths. When he was about 15, he left home and lived with an artist who taught him about all kinds of art. Perhaps his most famous painting is the Mona Lisa which you can see in the Louvre museum in Paris.

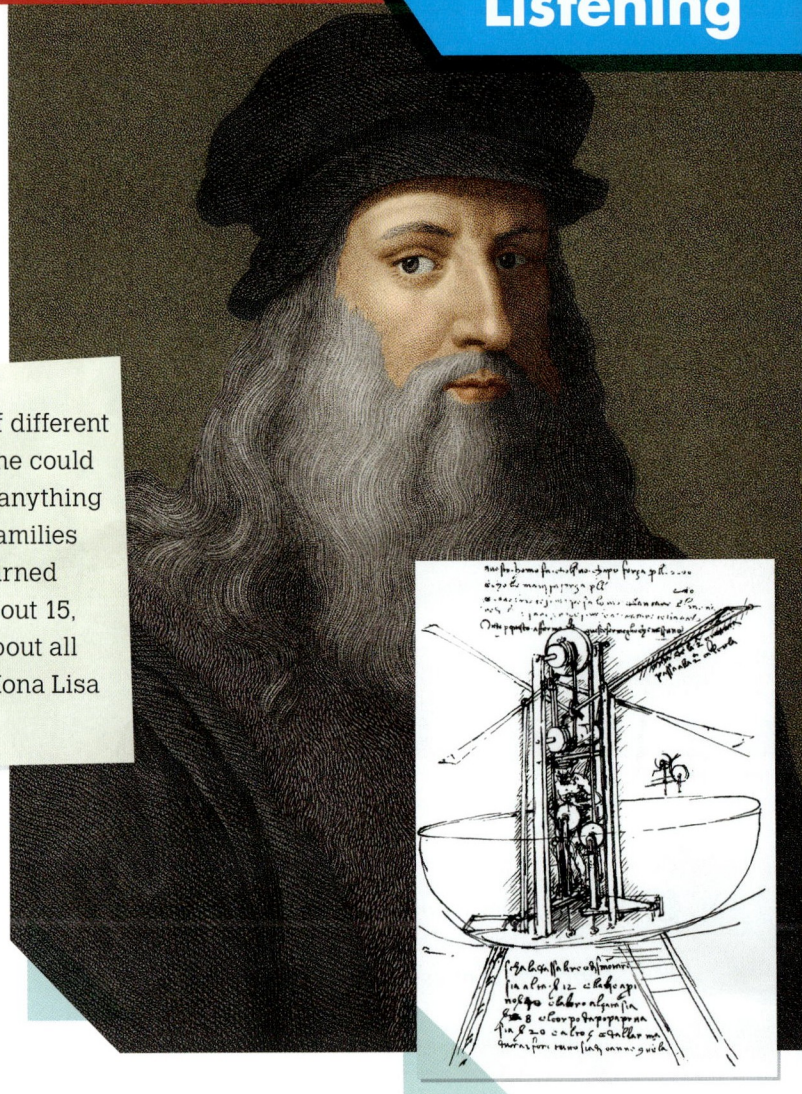

2 Look at the text again. Write the adverb form of these adjectives.

1 bad ....
2 good ....
3 beautiful ....

3 👁 Exam candidates often make mistakes with adverbs. Correct one mistake in each sentence.

1 I can write text messages very ~~quick~~. ......*quickly*......
2 I enjoyed the match because the players played wonderful. ....
3 My house is next to the museum; you can find it really easy. ....
4 I like this food when my mother cooks it because she can cook very good. ....
5 I liked the competition because it was funny! The team was playing very bad. ....

4 🔊 **24** You will hear five different people talking. Listen and circle the correct answer.

1 Day of school concert
   a Thursday   **b** Monday
2 Favourite subject
   a geography   **b** history
3 Time of maths class
   a 11.15   **b** 12.15
4 Cost of English book in school
   a £4.99   **b** £3.50
5 School trip to
   a water park   **b** zoo

💡 **Exam tip**

In this part of the exam you may hear two possible answers. Make sure you write the correct one.

☑ **Exam task**

🔊 **25** For each question, write the correct answer in the gap. Write one word or a number or a date or a time.

You will hear a teacher talking to her new class.

Leonardo Da Vinci School of Art and Drama
Nationality of teacher: ....*British*....
Lessons start at: **(1)** .... a.m.
Teacher's phone number: **(2)** ....
Everybody studies: **(3)** English, science and ....
Type of shoes for afternoon classes: **(4)** ....
Discount price of sweater: **(5)** £ ....

Speaking Part 1

💬 » Page 119

1 Work in pairs. Look at the picture. The students are meeting for the first time at an International Summer School. What questions do you think they ask?

> What's your name?

> Where are you from?

2 🔊 26 Listen to two students at the school and write down their questions.

3 Work in pairs. Ask and answer the six questions in Exercise 2.

> What's your name?

> I'm Maria.

4 🔊 27 Listen to two good exam candidates, Olga and Jorge, doing the first part of the Speaking exam. What questions does the examiner ask them? Tick (✓) the correct box.

	Olga	Jorge	Both
1 Do you study English at school?	☐	☐	☐
2 What other subjects do you study?	☐	☐	☐
3 Which subjects do you like best? Why?	☐	☐	☐
4 What do you like about your school?	☐	☐	☐

5 🔊 27 Listen again and complete Olga and Jorge's answers

Olga

1 Yes, I ......*do*...... We ....*have*...... English on Mondays, Wednesdays and Fridays.

2 I .... art and music.

3 Because I .... the piano well.

4 I .... a lot of friends there.

Jorge

5 I .... maths, art, music, history and science.

6 My friends – because we .... a lot of fun together

💡 Exam tip

Always give more than one-word answers, for example if the examiner asks 'Do you study English?', don't just say 'Yes'. Instead, say, 'Yes, it's my favourite subject,' or 'Yes, I study it at school.'

✓ Exam task

Work in groups of three. Take turns to be the examiner, Candidate A and Candidate B. The examiner asks the questions in Exercise 4. Candidate A and B answer the questions.

Remember to answer in full sentences; don't just repeat the language in the questions.

Reading & Writing Part 6
✎ >> Page 112

1 Read the email from Malik. How is he feeling? Why?

> ● ● ●
>
> **From:** Malik
>
> I'm singing and dancing in our school show tomorrow and I'm a little worried about it. Has your school got an end-of-year show? Can you sing or dance well? What other things do you do at the end of the year?

2 Work in pairs. Ask and answer the questions in Malik's email.

3 ◉ Exam candidates often make mistakes with their spelling. Read this reply to Malik's email and correct four more spelling mistakes.

> ● ● ●
>
> (Hi)
> ~~Hy~~ Malik,
>
> You shouldn't worry about the show becouse I know you can sing very well.
>
> Tommorow, we've got our school consert at 4 o'clock. I sing and dance very badly but I can play the guitar quite well. At the end of the year, we also go to a beatiful park with our teachers.
>
> Bye for now.

4 Read the exam task and answer the questions.

1 Do you have to write a note, an email or a message?
2 What three questions do you need to answer?

✓ Exam task

Read the email from your English friend, Lucy.

> ● ● ●
>
> **From:** Lucy
>
> I'm so happy. I finished all my exams yesterday. What is your school like? What subjects do you like best? Who is your favourite teacher?

Write an email to Lucy and answer the questions.

Write 25 words or more.

5 Read your exam task email again and complete the table with a tick (✓) or a cross (✗). If you put a tick next to each sentence, it is probably a good answer.

		✓	✗
1	I started and finished the email correctly.	☐	☐
2	I answered all three questions.	☐	☐
3	My spelling is correct.	☐	☐
4	My email is 25 words or more.	☐	☐

💡 Exam tip

Always check your spelling before you finish your note, email or message.

We had a great time!

What do you like doing when you're on holiday? Do you like adventure?

Do the quiz to find out.

1 When you're on holiday, do you prefer to ... ?
   a visit new countries
   b visit your own country
   c stay at home

2 When you're in a new country, do you ... ?
   a try to learn the language
   b speak English
   c speak your own language

3 Where do you stay?
   a at a campsite
   b with a family from the area
   c in a comfortable hotel

4 When you eat in a restaurant in a new place, do you ... ?
   a always eat something new
   b sometimes try a new dish
   c choose something you know

5 What is your dream holiday?
   a exploring the Amazon rainforest
   b visiting capital cities
   c having a rest

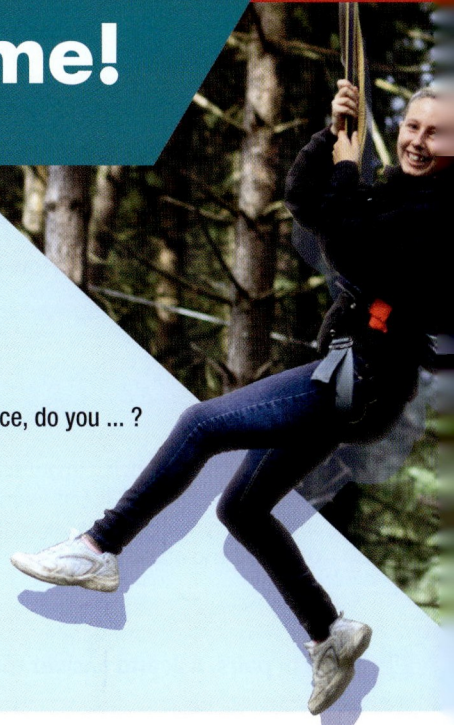

Grammar & Vocabulary

1 Work in pairs. Do the quiz.

2 Turn to page 133. Are the results true for you?

3 Complete the sentences with these verbs from the quiz.

> explore   have   learn   speak
> stay   try   visit

1 I would love to ..... explore ..... the lakes in North America.
2 When we go to a new country, we often have to .... English.
3 My mum and dad often go to restaurants to .... new dishes.
4 On the first day of the school holidays, I usually .... a rest.
5 My uncle wanted to go to Berlin but he didn't speak German so he decided to .... a new language.
6 When my cousin gets married, he wants to .... in a five-star hotel in Thailand.
7 My parents love museums so we often .... capital cities when we go on holiday.

Grammar – Past continuous

📝 ≫ Page 100

4 Read the text and match people 1–3 with the people in the picture.

Yesterday at 7.00 p.m. we were at the campsite. We were lucky, it wasn't raining. **(1)** Dad was building a fire, **(2)** my sister was reading a book and **(3)** Kevin and I were climbing a tree.

5 Underline four examples of the past continuous in the text in Exercise 4. Then answer the questions.

1 When was Dad building a fire?
2 Do we know when he started building a fire?
3 Do we know when he finished?

6 Choose the correct words to complete the email.

From: Sandra

We had a fantastic day at the hotel yesterday. At 11 o'clock, the sun **(1)** *was / were* shining and it **(2)** *wasn't / weren't* raining. My mum and dad **(3)** *was / were* reading their books, my little brother **(4)** *was / were* playing with his new friend and my cousin and I **(5)** *was / were* learning how to sail. What **(6)** *were / was* you doing at 11 o'clock yesterday?

Listening Part 5

1 Work in pairs. Look at the exam task and answer the questions.

1 Who is Victoria talking to? What about?
2 Who does Victoria talk about first?
3 Where did this first person stay on holiday?

💡 Exam tip

You will hear all the words in the first list (1–5) and they'll be in the same order. In the second list (A–H) you may hear the same word or a similar word but they won't be in the same order.

2 Here are some things that people take on holiday. Match each word (1–5) with a similar word (A–E).

1 money
2 clothes
3 a book
4 a camera
5 a mobile

A a dictionary
B €20
C photos
D a phone
E a jumper

3 🔊 28 Listen to Samuel talking to his sister about three friends. What did they forget to take on holiday? Choose one of the words (1–5) in Exercise 2 for each person.

1 Conor .... 2 Mark .... 3 Hanna ....

✅ Exam task

🔊 29 For each question, choose the correct answer.

You will hear Victoria and her dad talking about places to stay on holiday. Where did each of her friends stay?

Example:

0 Liam [C]

Friends		Places
1 Daniel	☐	A flat
2 Melissa	☐	B boat
3 Alba	☐	C campsite
4 Martin	☐	D castle
5 Olivia	☐	E farmhouse
		F friend's house
		G guest-house
		H hotel

4 Work in pairs. Ask and answer questions about the kinds of holidays you like. Use these words.

explore somewhere new   have a rest   learn the language   stay at a campsite
stay in a comfortable hotel   try new dishes   visit capital cities

Do you like staying at a campsite?

No, I don't. I prefer staying in a comfortable hotel.

Reading & Writing

Reading & Writing Part 4

1 Match the verbs (1–6) with the places and things (a–f). You can use some verbs more than once. Work in pairs and discuss your answers.

1 begin
2 pack
3 arrive at
4 pay for
5 catch
6 miss

a a flight / a bus
b a tour / a ticket
c a suitcase / a bag
d a train / a plane
e a hotel / the airport
f a journey / a holiday

You can *begin a tour*, so number 1 is b.

Yes, but you can't *begin a ticket*. I think *begin* goes with *a journey* or *a holiday*. That's f.

Exam tip

Look for words that often go together. Remember to read the words after the gap as well as the words before it.

2 Look at gap number 1 in the exam task. In the sentence before the gap, Melanie says she won a competition. Which word in question 1, A, B or C, means something that you can win in a *competition*?

Exam task

For each question, choose the correct answer.

Meet our competition winner, Melanie Dee from Manchester, England

I was doing my homework when the phone rang. A man told me I was the winner in a competition. The **(1)** .... was a trip to Guadeloupe with a tour group!

Dad took me to the airport. While he was driving, I checked the tickets for my **(2)** .... to Guadeloupe. A few hours later, I arrived in Pointe-à-Pitre, where I **(3)** .... the others in the group and we went to our hotel.

The language of Guadeloupe is French, but none of us could **(4)** .... it. So for the next few days, we had French lessons and visited interesting places in Pointe-à-Pitre. Then we travelled to an island called Terre-de-Bas and I **(5)** .... with the Dinart family in their house for two weeks.

I really enjoyed my time in Guadeloupe. My **(6)** .... thing was walking up La Soufrière mountain.

1 A gift   B prize   C present
2 A path   B way   C flight
3 A met   B had   C knew
4 A speak   B talk   C say
5 A visited   B stayed   C joined
6 A good   B excellent   C favourite

1 Did these people have a good time on holiday? Put a tick (✓) or a cross (✗).

1 We explored the market in Marrakech with a guide. It was amazing.
2 The weather was terrible. It was cold and cloudy.
3 We tried lots of new water sports. It was brilliant.
4 Our flight was delayed and then we missed the bus. The journey was tiring.
5 We went on a really interesting tour of Frankenstein Castle in Germany.
6 No, not really. We didn't do anything exciting. It was quite boring.
7 There was a clown at the hotel. He was really funny.

2 Complete the table with the adjectives from the box.

amazing	boring	brilliant	excellent	exciting
funny	interesting	terrible	tiring	wonderful

good ☺	bad ☹

3 👁 Exam candidates often make mistakes with adjectives of opinion. Correct one mistake in each of these sentences.

1 I'm ~~interesting~~ in London. I'm going to stay there for five days. ..interested..
2 I'd like to see that movie with you. It would be funny. ....
3 I saw the new film but it was very bored. ....
4 I'm really exciting about the concert. ....
5 I was shopping for clothes yesterday. I bought a wonderfull white coat. ....
6 It isn't a big bedroom but it's confortable and nice. ....

Grammar – Past simple & past continuous

📝 » Page 101

4 Look at these sentences from the article on page 50. Underline the verbs in the past simple and (circle) the verbs in the past continuous.

I was doing my homework when the phone rang …
While he was driving, I checked the tickets …

5 Complete the sentences with the past simple or past continuous form of the verb in brackets.

1 My mum .... (swim) in the sea with dolphins while she was in Florida.
2 We were fishing on the lake when it .... (start) to rain so we went home.
3 My dad found some money while he .... (pack) his suitcase.
4 My brother .... (study) in Ireland when he met his girlfriend.
5 My grandma .... (try) pizza for the first time while she was staying in Italy.
6 My friends saw some strange parrots while they .... (visit) the bird park.

6 Complete the questions with the past simple or past continuous form of the verb in brackets. Then write an answer that is true for you.

1 Was it raining when you .... (wake up) this morning?
2 What were you doing when the teacher .... (come) in?
3 What did you watch on TV while you .... (have) dinner yesterday?
4 Was your mum reading a book when you .... (get) home?

Reading & Writing Part 7

✎ » Page 114

1 Complete these sentences using *because*, *so* or *while*.

1 My mum doesn't like flying, ... we usually travel by car when we go on holiday.
2 We visited lots of museums .... we were in London.
3 One day, I would like to go to Africa .... I want to see wild elephants.
4 We went to Japan last month .... my uncle lives there.
5 Do you want to get something to eat .... we wait for the bus?
6 My cousin loves photography, ... he always takes his camera on holiday.

2 Look at the picture. Complete the story about it using *because*, *so* and *while*.

At the airport, Mum and my sisters decided to have a coffee **(1)** .... they were waiting for their flight. Mum thought the bill for their coffee was wrong **(2)**, ... she checked it carefully. Then she looked at the clock. 'Hurry up! Finish your coffee!' she said to them. 'Why?' they asked. **(3)** .... we're late!' answered Mum.

3 You can use either present or past tenses in Reading and Writing Part 7, but don't use both. Complete these sentences about the picture using *because*, *while* and *so* and a present tense.

1 A man is checking his phone ....
2 The man on the seat is tired, ...
3 One of the girls looks angry ....

4 Look at the pictures in the exam task. Work in pairs and talk about these questions. Try to use words like *because*, *while*, *so*, *and*, *when*, and *as* in some of your answers.

Picture 1 – Where were the teenagers? What were they doing?

Picture 2 – How did the girl with the phone feel? Why? How did the other teenagers feel?

Picture 3 – What did the boy do? Why?

Look at the three pictures.
Write the story shown in the pictures.
Write 35 words or more.

Speaking Part 2

💬 ≫ Page 120

1 Two exam candidates are talking about holidays.
Match their opinions with the pictures.

A I prefer spending time by the pool to going to the beach.

B I love camping, especially with my family. It's fun.

C I hate sightseeing because I get tired and bored.

2 Look at the examiner's question and Cari and Mehmet's answers.
Complete their answers using *like* or *would like*.

Examiner: What activities would you like to do on your next holiday, Cari?

Cari: Well, I **(1)** .... the beach, and on my next holiday I
(2) .... to learn to surf.

Examiner: Why?

Cari: Because I've seen people surfing on TV, and it looks fun.

Examiner: What about you, Mehmet? What activities would you like to do
on your next holiday?

Mehmet: I **(3)** .... going to the mountains, and I
(4) .... to go skiing again. It's so exciting!

3 🔊 **30** Now listen and check your answers.

4 Work in pairs and ask and answer the first question that the examiner
asked Cari and Mehmet. Remember to give a reason for your answer.

5 🔊 **31** Look at the first question in the exam task and listen to Cari's
answer. Which does she prefer, camping or staying in a hotel? What
reasons does she give?

💡 **Exam tip**

The examiner may ask you a
question about what you would
like to do in the future.

💡 **Exam tip**

The examiner might ask you a
question about what you prefer.

✓ **Exam task**

Work in pairs. Take turns to be the examiner and the candidate. The
examiner asks the questions and the candidate answers.

- When you go on holiday, do you prefer camping, or staying in a hotel? Why?
- Is it better to go on holiday with a few people, or a big group? Why?

9 What's on?

WHAT'S ON this weekend at the Centre?

FRI. 7.00 P.M.

Pop (1) ....*concert*.... – Tom Holt with his new guitar player.

SAT. 4.00 P.M.

Cinema 1 – The new adventure (2) .... with Daniel Radcliffe.

SAT. 6.00 P.M.

(3) .... competition – Which new young dancer will win first prize this year?

SUN. 3.00 P.M.

Beijing (4) .... – Clowns, music, dance and more.

And don't miss the photography (5) .... in the entrance hall.

Reading & Writing

Reading & Writing Part 3

1 Work in pairs. Complete the programme with words from the box. You do not need to use all the words.

> circus *concert* dance exhibition
> film party play

2 Read the blog about a film and answer the questions.

FILMS

I went to see Daniel Radcliffe's new film last week. I usually enjoy his films, and this was no different. I've read the book, so I knew the story. It's a pity the filmmakers decided to change the ending, but I still really enjoyed the film.

1 Underline what the writer says about the film. Does she think it was good or bad?

2 Now underline what the writer says about the story. What didn't she like? How do you know?

☼ Exam tip

There may be questions about someone's opinion. Read the text carefully and decide which answer, A, B or C, is giving the same opinion.

3 Look at question 1 in the exam task on page 55. Now look at the first paragraph of the text and answer these questions.

1 Hayley says that her bedroom is her classroom. Does she say that she chose this? Or that she likes it?

2 What does Hayley say about when she studies? Does she say that she likes this?

3 Does Hayley talk about the subjects she studies? Does she choose them?

4 Which is the correct answer for question 1?

✓ Exam task

For each question, choose the correct answer.

Thirteen-year-old Hayley Moore has lived in five different countries. 'It's because of my mum's job,' she explains. 'So I don't go to school; I study online. My computer's in my bedroom, so that's my classroom! I have to do all the same subjects as other students, but there's no timetable. That's the best thing. I can do my classes at any time.'

Hayley studies alone, but she often goes out with friends. 'Most people my age have hobbies like dancing or sports,' says Hayley. 'I've done those things too, but I thought they were boring. So when Mum told me about the circus club, I was really excited. It takes a long time to get there, but I love it.'

Hayley's favourite activity at the club is riding the unicycle – a bicycle with only one wheel. 'You sit on a seat just above the wheel, and there's nowhere to hold on! When I started, I fell off all the time, but that's the same for everyone. You just have to keep practising – which is what I do when I don't have homework!'

Next summer, when there are no lessons, Hayley is going to go to a circus summer camp. 'It's a camp for teenagers who are interested in the circus. I'm not going to see my family for a few weeks, but that's OK. I love the unicycle, but people from a real circus are going to teach us what they do in their shows, and I can't wait!'

1 Hayley likes studying online because she can choose
   A where to study.
   B when to study.
   C what to study.

2 Why did Hayley decide to try circus classes?
   A She didn't enjoy the other activities she tried.
   B The circus club isn't far from her home.
   C She didn't know many people her age.

3 What does Hayley say about riding the unicycle?
   A It was easier for her than for other people.
   B She needs to practise it more.
   C It was difficult at first.

4 Hayley is excited about the circus summer camp because
   A she is going to meet other teenagers who like circuses.
   B she is going to learn something new.
   C she is going to be in a show.

5 What is the best title for this text?
   A A new school for Hayley.
   B What Hayley does every summer.
   C Hayley's unusual life.

Grammar – *be going to*: positive & negative

📝 » Page 101

4 Look at the last paragraph of the exam task again and answer these questions in pairs.

1 What does Hayley say about her family?
2 What does she say about people from a real circus?
3 In both sentences, Hayley uses *be going to* + verb (without *to*). Why?

5 Complete the text with the correct form of *be going to* and the verb in brackets.

What are you going to do in the summer holidays?
Fourteen-year-old Madison Lee **(1)** _isn't going to study_ (not study) and she **(2)** .... (not meet) her friends. She **(3)** .... (dance) in a show with 30 other teenagers. They **(4)** .... (spend) three weeks practising hard and then they **(5)** .... (do) 70 shows in 25 different cities. Madison says, 'We **(6)** .... (have) fun but it **(7)** .... (not be) easy. I **(8)** .... (not see) my family or friends for two months. My mum and dad **(9)** .... (watch) our last show.'

Listening Part 4

1 Look at the picture. What do you think Fabio and Reyha are going to talk about?

2 🔊 **32** Listen to Fabio and Reyha talking about next weekend. Complete these sentences from their conversation.

   1 Is it going to be .... ?

   2 … they're playing ....

   3 The only concert I've ever been to was ....

3 🔊 **32** Now listen again, and check your answers. Where is the concert this year?

4 Look at the sentences in Exercise 2 again. Are Fabio and Reyha talking about a concert in the past, present or future in each sentence?

   1 ....

   2 ....

   3 ....

5 Look at question 1 in the exam task and answer the questions.

   1 What do you see at the cinema?

   2 Where do you usually go to see an exhibition?

💡 Exam tip

Read each question carefully. Does it ask about something happening in the past, the present or the future?

✓ Exam task

🔊 **33** For each question, choose the correct answer.

1 You will hear two friends talking about their plans for the weekend. What do they decide to do?

   A go to a concert

   B go to the cinema

   C go to an exhibition

2 You will hear a boy asking his friend Andres about yesterday evening. What was Andres doing?

   A playing a computer game

   B looking at an online video

   C watching a television programme

3 You will hear a girl leaving a message about a competition. What does the girl want to do in the competition?

   A sing

   B dance

   C play an instrument

4 You will hear two friends talking about going to a museum. How are they going to travel?

   A by car

   B by bus

   C by train

5 You will hear a boy talking about a concert. Why is he going to the concert?

   A The tickets are free.

   B His sister likes the group.

   C His friend is going to sing.

Speaking Part 1

💬 ≫ Page 119

1 Work in pairs. Decide what's on TV. Use some of the words from the box.

> cartoon music programme quiz show
> sports programme the news the weather

1 ....cartoon....

2 ....

3 ....

4 ....

2 Work in pairs. Discuss these questions.

1 How often do you watch TV?
2 What types of TV programmes do you like watching?
3 What types of TV programmes do you prefer *not* to watch? Why?

> 💡 **Exam tip**
>
> The examiner may ask you a question about things you are planning to do. Answer in full sentences with *going to*.

3 Put the words in the correct order to make questions.

1 have / going / you / are / What / to / dinner / for / tonight / ?
   What are you going to have for dinner tonight?
2 going / you / TV / What / watch / on / are / to / later / ?
3 see / film / Are / going / you / to / tomorrow / a / ?
4 weekend / you / to / do / at / What / are / going / the / ?
5 night / on / you / to / do / going / anything / special / Are / Saturday / ?
6 are / What / next / plans / week / your / for / ?

4 Work in pairs. Take turns to ask and answer the questions in Exercise 3.

📋 ≫ Page 101

5 🔊 34 Listen to an examiner asking Ella and Emir about their plans. Which question in Exercise 3 does he ask each one?

Ella ....
Emir ....

6 🔊 34 Listen again. Who answers their question better? Why?

> ✓ **Exam task**

Work in pairs. Take turns to be the examiner and the candidate. The examiner asks the questions and the candidate answers.

- What are you going to do this evening?
- What are your plans for the next school holidays?

Grammar & Vocabulary

Grammar – Infinitives & -ing forms

📋 » **Page 102**

1 Read the messages. What can you see at WOMAD this year?

Are you going to the WOMAD festival? What are you going to see?

I **love playing** the drums so I'm going to see the Kodo Drummers from Japan.

We **hope to see** the National Dance Company of Cambodia! Amazing dancers!

Is it **easy to buy** a ticket for the festival? I would like to see the jazz band from India.

I **enjoy watching** plays. Is there a theatre at WOMAD?

We're **interested in seeing** the circus. Is it good?

2 👁 Exam candidates often make mistakes with infinitives and -ing forms. Correct one mistake in each sentence.

1 I would love ~~going~~ to the cinema with you.   *to go*
2 My hobby is to play volleyball.
3 I hope see you soon.
4 I want invite you to visit me.
5 I need tell you something.
6 I would love helping you with the concert.

3 Complete Grant's email with the infinitive or -ing form of the verb in brackets.

From: Grant

Hi Gloria,

I'm at WOMAD and I'm having a fantastic time. Yesterday I enjoyed **(1)** .... (watch) a dance group from Senegal. My favourite band is going to play outdoors today. It's raining but I don't mind **(2)** .... (listen) to them in the rain. Today I want **(3)** .... (see) a hip-hop group from New Zealand. Why don't you come? It isn't difficult **(4)** .... (buy) a ticket. I'd love **(5)** .... (show) you around the festival. I hope **(6)** .... (hear) from you today!

Vocabulary – Word-building

4 We often add -er to a verb to make the word for the person who does the activity. Complete the sentences with the correct form of the word in capitals.

1 The ...*drummer*... played the drums really well.   DRUM
2 That book is brilliant but I can't remember the name of the ....   WRITE
3 I don't like discos very much because I'm not a good ....   DANCE
4 My brother loves taking photos. He's a great ....   PHOTOGRAPH
5 My mum often sings at home. She's an amazing ....   SING
6 My favourite .... is Van Gogh. I love all his paintings.   PAINT

5 Complete the words for more people. These words do not end with -er.

1 This person draws pictures. a..... ....
2 This person can play an instrument. m..... ....
3 If you are in a play, you are this. a..... ....
4 If you work in an office, write letters and make phone calls, you are this. s..... ....
5 This person writes about events in a newspaper. j..... ....

Reading & Writing Part 6

✏️ >> Page 112

1 Match the sentence beginnings (1–5) with the endings (a–e).

1 I don't like listening to hip-hop music
2 She wants to go to the circus
3 We're going to see a Japanese cartoon
4 We can watch the film at your house
5 I love going to the theatre

a but my friends don't like plays.
b or going to rock concerts.
c because she loves clowns.
d and after the cartoon, we're going to have pizza.
e or we can watch the film at mine. I don't mind.

2 Join the sentences with *and, or, but* or *because*.

1 I love listening to pop music. I love listening to reggae.
   I love listening to pop music and reggae.
2 We aren't going to the dance festival. There aren't any tickets left.
3 We can see a play. We can see a film.
4 Don't forget to see the Drummers of Burundi. Don't forget to bring your camera.
5 I don't like acting in plays. I like watching them.

☑️ Exam task

You want to ask your friend Sunita to go with you to a show.

Write a message to Sunita.

- **ask** Sunita **to go to a show** with you
- say **when** you would like to go
- tell Sunita **how to get there**.

Write 25 words or more.

3 Work in pairs. Anatoly has written the exam task answer. What do you think his teacher says to him?

> ✳ Hi,
> I'm ~~going~~ go to ~~to~~ see ~~headsup~~ Heads Up!
> ~~play~~ Why ~~dont~~ don't ~~it~~ you come?

4 Read Anatoly's complete exam task answer. Add *and, or, but* or *because* to improve his answer.

> Hi,
> I'm going to see Heads Up! **(1)** ....*because*.... they're brilliant.
> Why don't you come? We can go on Saturday **(2)** .... Sunday. We could go by bus **(3)** .... the train is quicker.
> Anatoly

💡 Exam tip

Use *and, or, but* and *because* to improve your writing.

5 Choose a show you would like to see from this unit or use your own ideas. Then write your own exam task answer.

6 Read your exam task answer and complete the table with a tick (✓) or a cross (✗). If you put a tick next to each sentence, it is probably a good answer.

		✓	✗
1	My writing is clear. I can read the answer.	☐	☐
2	It includes all three pieces of information.	☐	☐
3	I use *and, or, but* or *because*.	☐	☐
4	My answer is 25 words or more.	☐	☐

Listening

Listening Part 1

1   Match the places on Ned's map (A–H) with these words (1–8).

1 lake G	**3** gate	**5** hill	**7** wood
2 river	**4** path	**6** field	**8** farm

2   Work in pairs. Ned went to Drake's Farm yesterday and left his baseball cap there. Read his instructions and put a cross (✗) on the map in Exercise 1.

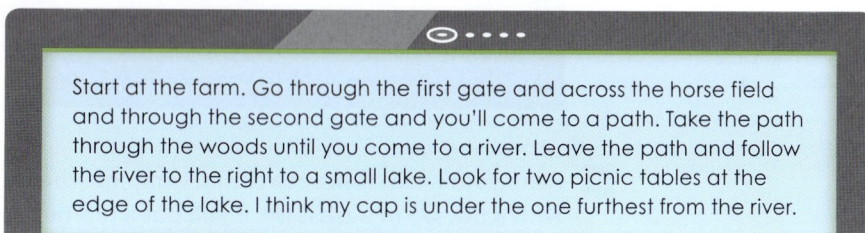

> Start at the farm. Go through the first gate and across the horse field and through the second gate and you'll come to a path. Take the path through the woods until you come to a river. Leave the path and follow the river to the right to a small lake. Look for two picnic tables at the edge of the lake. I think my cap is under the one furthest from the river.

☼ Exam tip

You may have to answer questions about where things are. Before you listen, look carefully at the three pictures.

3   Look at an example from an exam task below. Where is George's ball in each picture?

4   🔊 35   Now listen to the example. Why is A correct? What words do you hear?

Example: Where is George's ball?

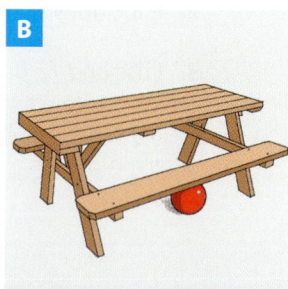

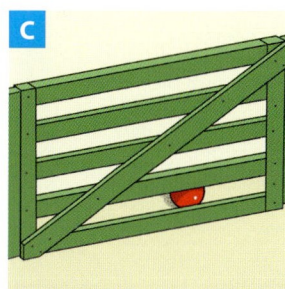

☑ Exam task

🔊 36 **For each question, choose the correct answer.**

1 Where will Joel and his family stay this year?

A

B

C

2 How much do Daniella's walking boots cost on the website?

A   **B**   **C**

3 What time does the park close today?

A

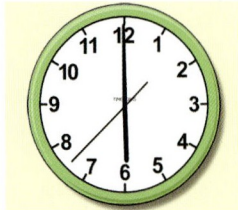
B

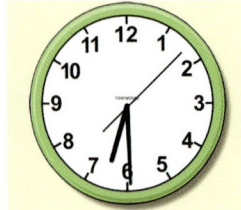
C

4 What will they do in the afternoon?

A

B

C

5 Where are Dad's keys?

A

B

C

Grammar – will / won't & may

📋 » **Page 103**

5 **Match the sentences (1–3) with their meaning (a–c).**

1 My cousin may see a lion. He's in Kenya at the moment.

a It's certain.

2 Mum won't see a lion today. She's working in London.

b It's possible.

3 We will see a lion. We're going to the zoo with our school.

c It's impossible.

6 👁 **Exam candidates often make mistakes when they use *will* and *may*. Correct the mistakes in these sentences.**

1 I ~~see~~ you soon!   *'ll see*

2 I am arrive at 11 o'clock.

3 I can't wait to see you tomorrow! What time will do you came here?

4 You maybe have problems getting to my house.

7 **Complete the conversation about a school trip with *will*, *won't* or *may* and the correct form of the verb in brackets.**

Chloe: I don't know what to wear tomorrow. Do you think it (1) ...*'ll rain*.. (rain)?

Alissa: It's possible, yes. It (2) .... (rain).

Chloe: How (3) .... (you / get) to school tomorrow morning by seven?

Alissa: I'm not sure. I (4) .... (go) by bus or my mum (5) .... (drive) me.

Chloe: Come to my house at 6.30. My dad says he (6) .... (take) us.

Alissa: Great! And don't worry. I (7) .... (not be) late.

Chloe: I think we (8) .... (have) fun there!

Reading & Writing

WEATHER

Reading & Writing Part 1

1 Label the pictures with words from the box. There are three words you do not need.

> cloud   fog   ice   rain   snow   storm
> sun   thunderstorm   wind

1 ......ice......   2 ....   3 ....

4 ....   5 ....   6 ....

2 Read the descriptions and write the season: *winter, spring, summer* or *autumn*.

When is the best time to visit your country?

Q: When is the best time to visit Sydney, Australia?

A: If you're there on 31st December, it'll be hot and sunny and you can join one of the many barbecues on the beach. Don't look for clouds in the sky, there won't be any!

Lucas, Sydney **(1)** .....summer.....

Q: What about Finland?

A: If you like snow and ice, you'll love Finland in December. Why don't you try ice-swimming in the lake? But don't forget that there's only six hours of light every day!

Eeva, Helsinki **(2)** ....

Q: And Seoul, the capital city of South Korea?

A: September to November is the best time when the skies are blue. Yes, it is a little cold but the leaves on the trees are orange, red and gold.

Mi Rae, Seoul **(3)** ....

Q: Is October a good time to visit Argentina?

A: Yes, it is! This is the best time for a visit. Winter finishes at the beginning of September, the temperature isn't too warm and the trees look beautiful with their blue flowers.

Diego, Buenos Aires **(4)** ....

3 Work in pairs. Imagine you are going to spend the day with friends at a large park in the countryside. What messages will you send and receive before you go? What notices will you see?

> Let's take a picnic.   **NO SWIMMING IN THE LAKE**

4 Compare your ideas with the notices and messages in the exam task on page 63.

💡 Exam tip

When you look for words which have a similar meaning, also remember to look for *not* + opposites, e.g. *cold* has a similar meaning to *not hot*.

5 Complete the notices and messages with these words.

> closed   cold   dry   easy   over   running

1 We don't serve hot drinks.

> ......Cold...... drinks only on sale here

2 The shop where Amelia wanted to buy her trainers wasn't open.

> Dad – Can you get my new trainers online? My favourite shoe shop was .... today, and that other one doesn't sell trainers.

3 Please walk.

> **NO ....**

4 Under-12s only.

> **Forbidden to 11s**

5 The party will be indoors because of wet weather.

> Dear Tennis Club Members, it's not as .... as we hoped, so we can't have our party outside. We'll use the hall. See you later.

6 Sara doesn't think there is time for the difficult walk.

> Tony, I talked about our trip with my sister, Sara. She thinks we should do the .... walk, as we only have two hours. Ben

✓ Exam task

For each question, choose the correct answer.

1
> Samuel, we can't go fishing today – the lake's covered in ice. Shall we go for a bike ride instead? Is ten o'clock too late? Alfonso

Why did Alfonso send this message?

A to find out if Samuel can go with him today
B to ask Samuel to give him ideas for today's activities
C to tell Samuel that they have to change their plan

2
> The Adventure Park is closed this week while we add more fun activities.

A You can't use the adventure park as they are repairing some parts of it.
B When the adventure park opens again it will be even better than before.
C There are other activities you can do while the adventure park is shut.

3
> Sara – about the forest walk. Dad says it isn't too hard for us, but he'll come anyway for the beautiful views and the fresh air! Amelia

Sara's dad will go with the girls because

A he is worried that the walk is difficult for them.
B the walk will be easy for him.
C he wants to walk in the countryside.

Grammar – First conditional

🗒 ≫ Page 104

6 Work in pairs. Look at the picture and answer the questions.

1 Is the gate open? 2 Where are the cows?
3 Is the farmer angry? Why? / Why not?

Boy: What does this notice mean?
Girl: If the gate's open, the cows will run away.
Boy: The farmer won't be pleased if the cows run away.
Girl: That's right.

4
> Park Café
> Today's special offer:
> Free guidebook for customers whose bill is over £20

A You will get a guidebook if you spend enough today.
B If you show your guidebook, your food will be cheaper.
C You can buy guidebooks for less than usual today.

5
> Pedro – I called that little shop in the park. It's open between 10 a.m. and 3 p.m. but it only sells snacks. Let's take a picnic. Monica

Monica thinks they should take a picnic because the shop

A doesn't open at lunchtime.
B doesn't sell much food.
C isn't very big.

6
> **KYLE RIVER**
> Please be careful when crossing this bridge in wet weather. DON'T RUN.

A You might fall if it has rained.
B The bridge is closed because of the rain.
C This is the only place to cross the river in rainy weather.

7 Complete the conversation between the girl and boy. Use the first conditional and the verb in brackets.

Tess: Let's go for a walk in the hills.
Leo: But if it rains, we **(1)** 'll get (get) wet.
Tess: If it rains, we **(2)** .... (not get) wet because we **(3)** .... (find) a cave.
Leo: What **(4)** .... (we / do) if we **(5)** .... (find) insects and bears in the cave?
Tess: If we **(6)** .... (find) insects and bears, we **(7)** .... (not stay) in the cave!
Leo: What will we do if we get lost?
Tess: We **(8)** .... (phone) my mum if we **(9)** .... (get) lost.
Leo: What will we do if she **(10)** .... (not answer) her phone?
Tess: We **(11)** .... (call) my dad.

Reading & Writing

✎ >> Page 114

1 👁 Exam candidates often make mistakes with the spelling of words. Look at this story. Correct the <u>underlined</u> spelling mistakes.

> A family went for a walk in the forest. It was a cold day, so they all wore warm <u>trowsers</u>, boots and jackets. The family tried to use the map <u>wich</u> they had with them, but they got lost. The girl had her <u>mobail</u>, so she used it to help them find the way. The mother said to her daughter: 'I'm so glad that you <u>brort</u> your phone with you!'

2 Read the story in Exercise 1 again and answer these questions.

1 Where were the family? Why did they wear warm clothes?
2 Why did the girl use her phone to find the way?
3 How did the mother feel at the end?

3 Look at the people in the pictures in the exam task.
In pairs, answer these questions.

1 Picture 1: Where were the teenagers? What were they doing?
2 Picture 2: What did the teenagers see? What happened to the sheep? Why? How did the farmer feel? Why?
3 Picture 3: What happened next? What did the teenagers do?
4 Which words can you use to connect the different parts of the story together?

💡 **Exam tip**

Remember to write about what the people did. You may also be able to write about how they felt, and why they did things.

☑ **Exam task**

Look at the three pictures.
Write the story shown in the pictures.
Write 35 words or more.

4 When you have finished, read your story, and make sure you have done everything on this list.

- Did you write about all of the pictures?
- Did you say what the people were doing in the story?
- Did you spell all of the words correctly?
- Did you connect your ideas with words like *and, because, so, then*?

Speaking Part 2
>> Page 120

1 🔊 37 Look at the pictures of activities that you can do on an adventure weekend. Listen to Luisa and Alexander talking about the activities. Who talks about each activity?

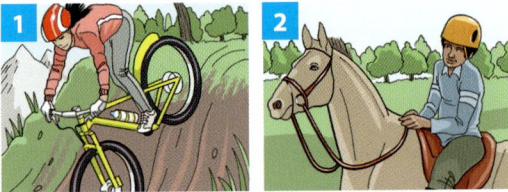

2 Alexander talked about an activity that he didn't like. Which one was it? Why doesn't he like it?

3 Work in pairs. Can you think of words to describe the activities in the pictures in Exercise 1?

interesting, difficult

4 🔊 38 Listen to an examiner asking Luisa and Alexander about the first activity in Exercise 1.
Do they use the words you thought of?

5 Alexander says 'I don't agree. I think it looks really exciting.' Complete the table with the expressions for agreeing and disagreeing from the box.

I agree.   I don't agree.   Probably, yes.   No, I don't think so.
Not really.   Not for me.   Yes, I do.   Yes, I think it is.   I disagree.

agreeing	disagreeing
I agree.	I don't agree.

💡 Exam tip

Remember, you can agree or disagree with the other student. Give reasons for your opinion.

6 Work in pairs. Ask and answer questions about the other activities in Exercise 1. Use expressions from Exercise 5 to agree and disagree with each other.

I think horse riding is dangerous.

I don't agree. It's safe, but it is expensive.

✓ Exam task

Now, in this part of the test, you are going to talk together. Here are some pictures that show different activities that you can do in the countryside.

a Do you like these different activities? Say why or why not.
b Answer one question at least:
- Do you think walking is boring?
- Do you think wind-surfing is difficult?
- Do you think climbing is dangerous?
- Do you think swimming in a lake is exciting?
- Do you think fishing is fun?
- Which of the activities do you like best?

Reading & Writing

Reading & Writing Part 4

1 What do you know about the human body? Read the questions and choose the best answer.

1 How fast does your hair grow?
  a 1.25 cm a day
  b 1.25 cm a month
  c 1.25 cm a year

2 How long should you spend brushing your teeth?
  a 1 minute
  b 2 minutes
  c 2 to 3 minutes

2 Read the text and check your answers.

Q My mum has just cut my hair and it looks terrible. She says, 'Don't worry! It'll soon grow.' How fast does hair grow?

A Most people's hair grows 1.25 cm a month. So, in four months, your hair will be 5 cm longer!

Q I've just been to the dentist and she says I should brush my teeth more. How long should I spend brushing my teeth?

A Brush them for two to three minutes at least twice a day. And have you bought a new toothbrush this year? You should change your brush about every three months.

3 Complete the table with the words from the box.

| arm back ear eye face foot hand |
| leg mouth neck nose stomach tooth |

one	two	more than two
face	arm	

Grammar – Present perfect; *just*

📋 » Page 105

4 Work in pairs. <u>Underline</u> three examples of the present perfect in the text in Exercise 2. What form of the verb always comes after *have* or *has*?

5 👁 Exam candidates often make mistakes with the past participle. Correct one mistake in each of these sentences.

1 I've ~~palyed~~ a lot of football today. played
2 I've desided to buy a new phone.
3 We've eatten some sweets and now we feel sick.
4 I have just wathed a football match with my parents.
5 He has attened a first-aid course.
6 I've forgetten to tell you about my new haircut.

6 Put the words in order to make sentences.

1 leg / John / broken / 's / his / .
 John's broken his leg.

2 lost / my / 've / tablet / I / .
 ....

3 finished / you / homework / your / Have / ?
 ....

4 stopped / hasn't / all morning / raining / It / .
 ....

5 the / Sue / book / read / Has / ?
 ....

7 Complete the sentences with *just* and the correct form of the verb in brackets.

1 Why has your brother stopped playing football?
 He 's just hurt .... (hurt) his foot.

2 My little sister's crying. She .... (cut) her finger.

3 I can't go swimming now. I .... (have) my lunch.

4 Sorry we're late, but we .... (visit) the dentist.

5 I don't want any chocolate. I .... (brush) my teeth.

Grammar – *yet / already*

📝 ≫ **Page 105**

8 Lucas and Saskia are planning a party. Read their conversation and put a tick (✓) or a cross (✗) next to the activities they have or haven't done.

Lucas: Have you decided on a date yet?
Saskia: Yes, the 5th and I've already booked the hall.
Lucas: Thanks, Saskia. That's great!
Saskia: But I haven't invited our friends yet! Can you do that?

> TO DO:
> Decide on a date ✔
> Book the hall
> Invite our friends

9 Complete Lucas's message by choosing *yet* or *already*.

> ● ● ●
>
> I'm so excited about our party. I have
> **(1)** *yet / already* invited our friends and my mum
> has **(2)** *yet / already* made a cake for us. Have you
> seen it **(3)** *yet / already*? It's amazing!
>
> I think we'll have a great time. We haven't talked
> about the food **(4)** *yet / already*. Shall we talk
> tomorrow?

10 The text in the exam task is about glasses. Look at the first sentence, and the three options in question 1. Answer these questions.

1 Can you **hold** a pair of glasses?
2 Can you **wear** a pair of glasses?
3 Can you **take** a pair of glasses?
4 What's the difference between holding, wearing and taking glasses?
5 Which is the correct answer for question 1, A, B or C?

> 💡 **Exam tip**
>
> Read the three options, A, B and C, and think about the difference between them before you choose the right word for the text.

✓ Exam task

For each question, choose the correct answer.

A short history of glasses

People haven't always **(1)** .... glasses. History books say there weren't any reading glasses when the Italian writer Seneca was born in 4BC, for example. So how did people with bad eyes read without them? Seneca looked **(2)** .... a drinking glass!

We've known for a long time that the sun can **(3)** .... our eyes. The Chinese first used sunglasses about 2,000 years ago. In the north of Canada, the sunlight on the snow is very strong in spring when the sun is **(4)** .... in the sky. People put **(5)** .... of wood over their eyes before they had sunglasses there.

People didn't start to use glasses to see better until much later. People **(6)** .... that the first pair of glasses was made in Italy in about 1284.

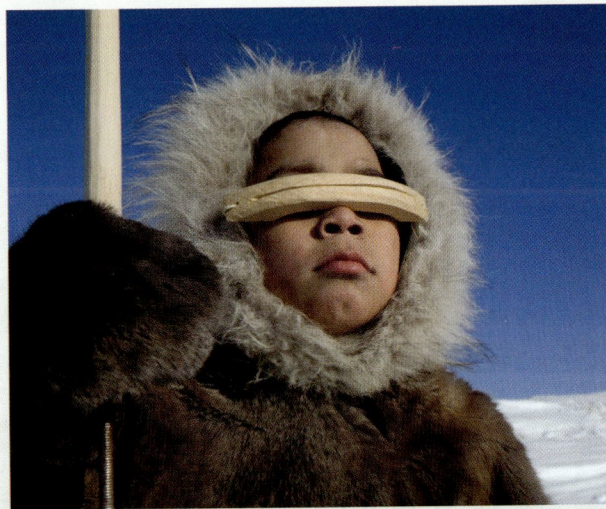

	A		B		C	
1	held		worn		taken	
2	through		across		between	
3	break		fail		hurt	
4	high		deep		tall	
5	areas		pieces		sides	
6	describe		believe		understand	

Reading & Writing

Reading & Writing Part 2

1 Complete the conversation with the words from the box. There are three extra words you don't need.

> broken   cut   down   hot
> hurts   matter
> plaster   temperature   ~~well~~

Dan: Mum, I don't feel (1) ....*well*........
Mum: What's the (2) ....?
Dan: My head (3) .... and I feel (4) ....
Mum: I think you've got a (5) ....
You should lie (6) ....

2 Read the text about Maria and the sentences below. Are the sentences true (T) or false (F)? For each sentence, underline the part of the text where you can find the information you need.

> Maria didn't go to school on Monday because she didn't feel well. She had a headache and a temperature. Her mum thought she probably had a cold. Maria stayed in bed all day. She was bored and she missed her friends. On Tuesday she felt better, and her mum said, 'I think you're well enough for school today.' Maria was glad.

1 Maria didn't go to school for two days.
2 Her mother was sure that Maria had a cold.
3 Maria enjoyed staying in bed on Monday.
4 She felt worse on Tuesday.
5 She was happy to return to school when she was better.

💡 Exam tip

Read the questions carefully. Sometimes you will see a word from a question in one of the texts, but it might not be the correct answer.

✓ Exam task

For each question, choose the correct answer.

		Alessio	Selim	Esteban
1	Who has spent the night in a hospital?	A	B	C
2	Who offered to help someone when he was in the hospital?	A	B	C
3	Who felt scared when he first entered the hospital?	A	B	C
4	Who made a friend when he was in the hospital?	A	B	C
5	Who thinks it's boring to be in hospital?	A	B	C
6	Who learned something new in the hospital?	A	B	C
7	Who is interested in being a doctor?	A	B	C

A trip to hospital

Alessio

I've never stayed in a hospital, but about a month ago I visited my friend there. He was in a room with lots of other people. I was afraid just before we went into the room, but then I saw my friend. He was smiling and didn't look ill. The doctors and nurses were really kind and my friend got better quickly. He said being in hospital was OK, but I'm not sure. There's nothing to do except sleep and watch TV.

Selim

I went to the hospital when my little sister was born. Mum stayed there for a night and we visited the next day. Dad asked me if I was scared about going to a hospital, but I was just excited about meeting my sister. The hospital was interesting. The doctor told me that little babies can't see well, which I didn't know before. I asked Mum if she wanted me to wash the baby with her, but we did that when we took her home.

Esteban

I had to go to hospital when I broke my leg. I was there for two days. I met another boy there, and we talked and played together so we didn't get bored. I taught him to play cards. I still see him sometimes. My leg hurt, but the doctors gave me medicine to take the pain away and showed me pictures of my leg, called X-rays. I think I'd like to do their job. It's good to help people when they're ill.

Reading & Writing Part 6

✏️ ≫ Page 112

Grammar – Present perfect with *for* & *since*

📝 ≫ Page 106

1 Read the conversation and answer the questions.

Vadim: You're very quiet. What's the matter?
Anya: I've had toothache for three days.
Vadim: Have you been to the dentist yet?
Anya: No, I haven't been to the dentist since 2015.
I'm afraid of dentists.

1 When did Anya's tooth start hurting?
2 Does it hurt now?
3 Why hasn't she been to the dentist?

2 Choose the correct word to complete the sentences.

1 I've had long hair *for / since* January.
2 I've known my dentist *for / since* 2014.
3 My dad has worn glasses *for / since* four years.
4 We've lived near the hospital *for / since* six months.
5 I've felt tired *for / since* nine o'clock.

3 Match the questions (1–6) with the correct answers (a–f).

1 How do you keep fit?
2 Why did you go to the doctor's?
3 What do you do when you have a headache?
4 Who are you going to visit at the hospital?
5 How long have you had a cold?
6 When did you hurt yourself?

a For about three days.
b I go running every day.
c I did it yesterday.
d My little brother.
e I had a pain in my leg.
f I take some medicine.

> **💡 Exam tip**
>
> Remember, you may be asked to answer questions starting with words like *What*, *Where*, *When* or *How*. Look at the question words carefully and make sure you answer all three questions.

4 Use the questions and answers in Exercise 3 to write complete sentences.

I keep fit by going running every day.

☑️ Exam task

Read the email from your English friend, Robyn.

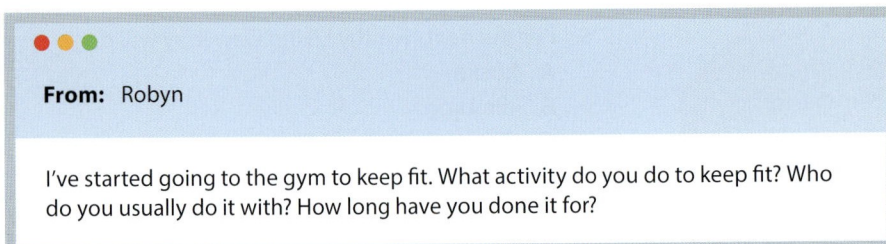

From: Robyn

I've started going to the gym to keep fit. What activity do you do to keep fit? Who do you usually do it with? How long have you done it for?

Write an email to Robyn. Write 25 words or more.

Listening Part 3

1 Work in pairs. Tick (✓) the correct word for each picture.

1	afraid ✓	2	thirsty ☐	3	happy ☐	4	angry ☐	5	sick ☐	6	great ☐
	tired ☐		hungry ☐		bored ☐		sorry ☐		glad ☐		unhappy ☐

2 Read the situations and answer the questions. Use some of the words in Exercise 1.

Does everybody feel the same?

We'd like to know how our readers feel in different situations. Please complete our questionnaire before 3rd February and you can read the results in March.

1 You've just finished your school exams and you think you've done well. How do you feel?

2 It's lunchtime and you haven't eaten yet. Your mum asks you to go to the supermarket. How do you feel?

3 You've just won first prize in a sports competition. How do you feel?

4 You haven't phoned your best friend for a few days and now you've heard he's/she's ill. How do you feel?

5 You're watching a frightening film alone. You've just heard a strange noise. How do you feel?

1 *I feel happy and a little tired.*

💡 Exam tip

You often hear information about all three answers. When you choose the correct answer, think about why the other two answers are incorrect.

3 🔊 **39** Look at question 1 in the exam task. Listen to the first part of the conversation. Which is the correct answer, A, B or C? Why are the other answers wrong?

✅ Exam task

🔊 **40** For each question, choose the correct answer.

You will hear Alissa talking to her friend Joey about a Healthy Living Day at a sports centre.

1 How did Alissa feel at the end of her day at the sports centre?
- **A** ill
- **B** tired
- **C** thirsty

2 How much did Alissa pay for the Healthy Living Day?
- **A** £10
- **B** £15
- **C** £20

3 Joey would like to do a Healthy Living Day because he thinks
- **A** he might make new friends.
- **B** he should do more exercise.
- **C** he needs to try a different sport.

4 Joey will go to the Healthy Living Day on
- **A** 28th May.
- **B** 14th June.
- **C** 5th July.

5 For the next Healthy Living Day, Joey will do
- **A** hockey.
- **B** climbing.
- **C** skateboarding.

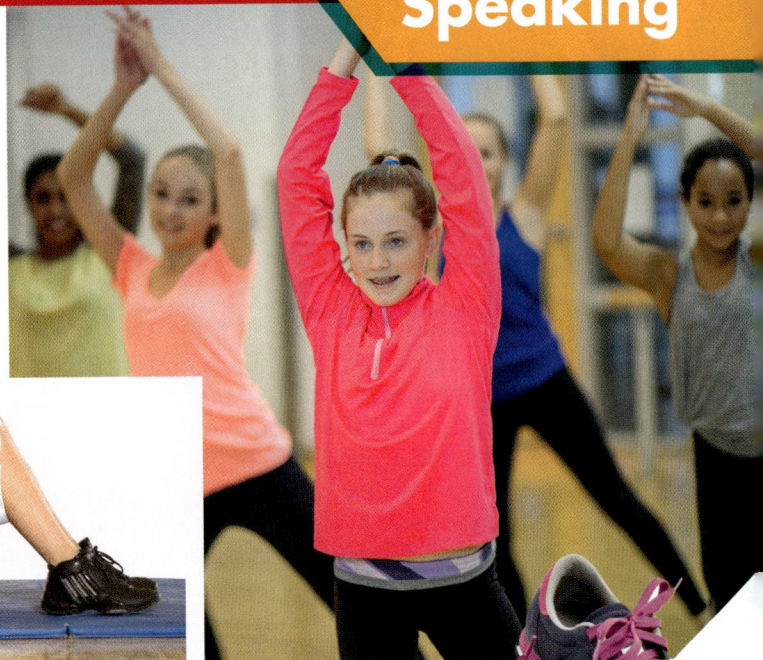

Speaking Part 1

💬 ≫ Page 119

1 Brody has just joined a health and fitness club and is talking to his new trainer. Look at the form. What questions do you think the trainer will ask Brody?

Glenview Health & Fitness Club

Young People's Programme

Name: (1) ......Brody......

Surname: (2) ....

Address: (3) ...., Petersdale

Number of years at this address: (4) ....

Date of birth: (5) ....

School: (6) ....

Favourite sports: (7) ....

Favourite food: (8) ....

Health problems: (9) ....

Free-time activities: (10) ....

a What's your name? ✓

b .... ☐

c .... ☐

d .... ☐

e .... ☐

f .... ☐

g .... ☐

h .... ☐

i .... ☐

j .... ☐

2 🔊 41 Listen to Brody talking to his new trainer and complete the information (1–10) on the form.

3 🔊 41 Work in pairs. Complete the trainer's questions (a–j) in Exercise 1. Then listen again and check your answers.

4 🔊 42 Listen to an examiner asking Ariana some questions. Tick (✓) the examiner's questions (a–j) in Exercise 1.

5 🔊 42 Listen again. What does Ariana say when she doesn't understand the examiner's questions? Tick (✓) all the phrases you hear.

I'm sorry. I don't understand. ☐
Pardon? ☐
Sorry? ☐
Can you say that again, please? ☐

💡 **Exam tip**

If you don't understand a question in Part 1, ask the examiner to say it again.

✓ **Exam task**

Student A is the examiner. Ask questions (a–j) in Exercise 1.

Student B is the candidate. Answer the questions. If you don't understand a question, use one of the expressions in Exercise 5.

PC Bangs

In South Korea, computers, tablets and smartphones are a very important part of the culture. According to recent studies, almost all of the population go online at least once a week and around 50% of people spend more than 14 hours a week on the internet. As with other countries, this is often to send messages, chat with friends, shop online, post social media updates, or download films and TV shows. However, online games are particularly important in South Korea with over 25 million gamers (over half of the population) playing mobile, video or online multi-player games.

But where do South Koreans go when they want to use a really fast computer to play an online multi-player game? For most Koreans gamers, the answer is a PC Bang. Bang is a Korean word for room so a PC Bang is a kind of internet café or games centre with hourly fees of about $1 per hour. PC Bangs are particularly popular with teenagers as social meeting places.

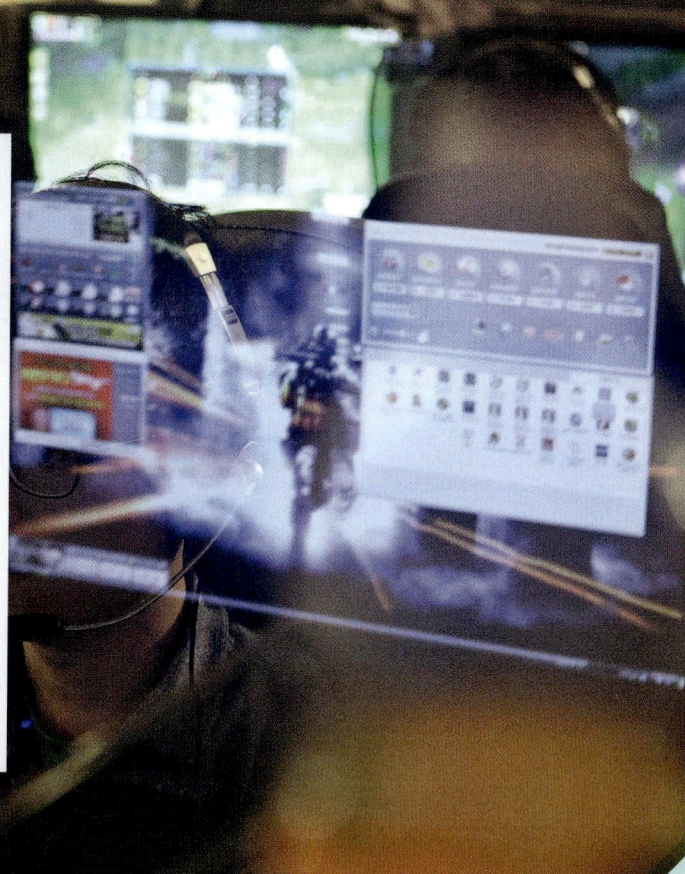

Listening

Listening Part 5

1 Read the text about young people from South Korea. What is a PC Bang? Have you got something similar in your country?

2 Choose the correct verbs to complete these questions. Use the text in Exercise 1 to help you.

1 Do you *go / use* the internet every day?
2 How much time do you *take / spend* online per week?
3 How many messages do you *make / send* per day?
4 When was the last time you *posted / updated* something on social media such as Facebook and Twitter?
5 Have you *downloaded / saved* any mobile games for your smartphone? If so, which ones?
6 Do you *play / practise* any multi-player games with friends or family?

3 Work in pairs. Ask and answer the questions in Exercise 2.

☀ Exam tip

You may hear two of the answers (A–H) for each person (1–4). Listen for words like *but*, *instead* and *now* as these will help you to choose the correct one.

4 🔊 **43** Listen to Susie talking to her brother about her friends. Each friend has just got something new. Tick (✓) the correct word.

1	Leo	laptop	✓	mobile phone ☐
2	Elsa	DVD ☐		printer ☐
3	Callum	games console ☐		DVD ☐
4	Sunita	games console ☐		DVD ☐

5 Read the exam task on page 73. Who is Tasha talking to? What about?

✓ Exam task

🔊 44 For each question, choose the correct answer.

You will hear Tasha talking to a friend about her family. What is each person's favourite thing?

Example:

0 Dad ☐ A

People		Things
1 Mum	☐	**A** CD player
2 Sister	☐	**B** digital camera
3 Brother	☐	**C** DVD player
4 Grandmother	☐	**D** laptop
5 Grandfather	☐	**E** mobile phone
		F PC
		G tablet
		H TV

Grammar – The passive: present simple

📝 » Page 107

6 Look at the pictures and answer the questions.

1 My friends often send me messages.   2 I'm sometimes sent funny videos.

1 Do we know who sends messages to the boy?
2 Do we know who sends the funny videos? Is it important?
3 Which sentence is in the passive?
4 How do we form the passive?

7 Complete the definitions with the present passive form of the verbs in brackets. Then write the correct word.

> ~~camera~~   email address   internet
> keyboard   mouse   screen

1 Photos ..are taken.. (take) with this. ...camera....
2 Films .... (watch) on this. ....
3 This .... (need) to write on a computer. ....
4 Music .... (download) from here. ....
5 This .... (move) and it .... (click) to do things on the computer screen. ....
6 Messages .... (send) to you here. ....

8 Complete the text with the present passive form of the verbs in brackets.

WHAT IS *Instagram*?

Instagram is an app which **(1)** .... (use) to share photos and videos with friends. It's easy to join Instagram; the app **(2)** .... (download) for free onto a smartphone and you then sign up using your email address or phone number. Often a real name **(3)** .... (not use) – a lot of people use a nickname. On Instagram, the people who see our photos or videos **(4)** .... (not call) 'friends'. They **(5)** .... (know) as 'followers' because they follow our posts. Many famous people **(6)** .... (follow) on Instagram. Some famous pop stars have over 100 million followers!

Reading & Writing

1 Work in pairs. Read the description. Do you study ICT at your school?

> ICT /ˌaɪ siːˈtiː/
> Information and Communication Technology
>
> The use of computers and other new technology to save and send information. It's taught as a subject in schools in the UK.

2 Read question 1 in the exam task and underline the important words. Then answer these questions.

1 What's the correct answer? Underline the important information in the text.
2 Why is *C Gloria* not the correct answer?

> 💡 **Exam tip**
>
> When you look for information about the words you have underlined, don't just choose a person because their paragraph includes the same words.

> ✓ **Exam task**

For each question, choose the correct answer.

		Berta	Elif	Gloria
1	Who studies ICT as a school subject?	A	B	C
2	Who never uses school books during lessons?	A	B	C
3	Who does a sport with friends after school?	A	B	C
4	Who says schools won't use books in the future?	A	B	C
5	Who has to go to another classroom to go online?	A	B	C
6	Who doesn't enjoy using technology?	A	B	C
7	Who likes studying with other people?	A	B	C

Computers and school

A

Berta

We use computers and other technology in almost every class at school, and everybody is given a tablet computer to use. We also do ICT every Wednesday. Nobody buys textbooks any more, but we still read books in our free time. In the future, I don't think people will have to go to school. We'll have all our lessons online at home and that will give us more time to do sport with our friends.

B

Elif

We aren't taught ICT at our school. If we need to use the internet, the teacher takes us to the computer room, but we mostly use books in class. I don't mind that because I don't really like spending my time on computers or things like that. I prefer to finish my homework quickly and then go out skating with my friends. I'm sure that in the future people will use computers to study even more than now.

C

Gloria

We don't study ICT as a school subject because it's part of every class and we can go online in all the classrooms. I often use the internet to do my homework, too. My mum says we never use our school books but this isn't true. It's just that we use technology, too. I think the lessons of the future will be online, without books. But I hope we still go to school, because I might miss my friends if I have to study alone at home.

Grammar – The passive: past simple

📝 » **Page 107**

1 Work in pairs. Match the pictures (A–C) with the descriptions (1–3).

A

B

C

1 Music **was played** on this before mobiles **were sold**.
2 This was one of the first portable computers. It **was carried** from one office to another.
3 This **was used** for calling people. It's an old telephone!

2 Write complete sentences in the past simple passive.

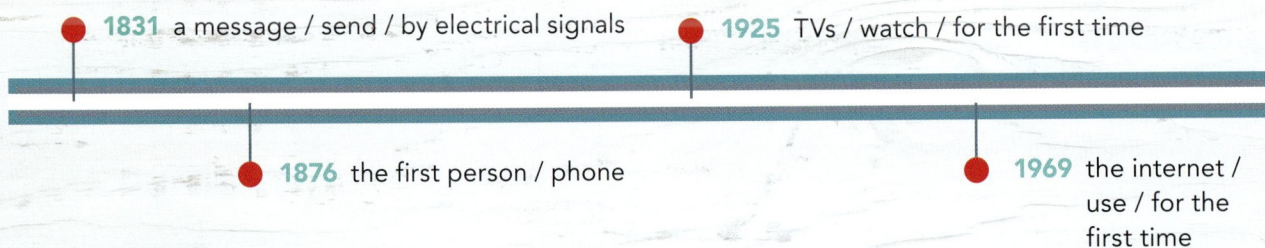

● **1831** a message / send / by electrical signals   ● **1925** TVs / watch / for the first time

● **1876** the first person / phone   ● **1969** the internet / use / for the first time

1 .... A message was sent by electrical signals in 1831. ....
2 ....
3 ....
4 ....

3 👁 Exam candidates sometimes make mistakes with the present and past simple passive. Correct one mistake in each sentence.

1 My old games console ~~is~~ broken last year. _was_
2 There is a new model of DVD I would like to buy. It made in Japan. ....
3 The name of a woman was writed on a piece of paper. ....
4 I bought a new one because my old chair broke by my little brother. ....
5 This present gave to me by my German friend. ....
6 The building is made in 1960. ....

4 Active or passive? Choose the correct answers to complete the conversation.

Kirsty: I'm really tired. I **(1)** *woke / was woken* up by my sister at 7 a.m.
Charlie: Why **(2)** *did she do / was she done* that?
Kirsty: She **(3)** *gave / was given* a games console and she **(4)** *decided / was decided* to play loud games this morning.
Charlie: Oh, dear! I **(5)** *send / was sent* two free tickets to 'The Technology Show' yesterday. **(6)** *Do you want / Are you wanted* to come with me?
Kirsty: Yes, please! I **(7)** *love / am loved* technology shows! But it **(8)** *don't call / isn't called* 'The Technology Show' any more. Now it's 'Futures'.

Speaking

Speaking Part 2

💬 ≫ Page 120

1 🔊 **45** Listen to Deniz and Silvia talking about music. Answer the questions.

1 What three different ways of listening to music do they talk about?
2 Which of the three ways does Deniz think sounds best?

2 🔊 **45** Complete this part of Deniz and Silvia's conversation. Listen again.

Silvia: But what about the music? How does it sound?

Deniz: Well, maybe not .... good .... a download from the internet, but I still like it.

3 We can use *as … as* to say that two things are the same, or *not as … as* to say that two things are different. Complete the sentences with words from the box.

> dark   big   fun   interesting   fast   heavy

1 When my parents were younger, computers took a long time to start. They weren't as .... as they are now.
2 Is your phone screen as .... as mine? It looks the same size.
3 I don't like this computer game. It's not as much .... as the others.
4 What's wrong with your tablet? The screen isn't usually as .... as that!
5 Is your phone as .... as mine? It looks lighter.
6 Let's see if the information on this website is as .... as on that one.

4 Work in pairs. Ask and answer these questions.

1 Do you prefer watching films on a laptop or on your phone? Why?
2 What's more fun, making videos, or watching videos that other people have posted online? Why?
3 What's your favourite piece of technology? Why?

💡 **Exam tip**

You may be asked which of two things you think is better. Say how they're different to explain your answer.

✓ **Exam task**

Take turns to be the examiner and the candidate. The examiner reads the question and the candidate answers.

1 Do you prefer phoning people, or sending messages? Why?
2 Do you like using your phone to take photos? Why? / Why not?
3 Is it better to play computer games alone, or with other people?

Reading & Writing Part 5

1 Read the descriptions and write the words.

1 It's used to tell the time and to wake us up.
a a l a r m c l o c k.

2 People put this on a mobile phone. It's often made of leather or plastic. c ....

3 You turn it on and you use it for reading when it's dark.
l ....

4 You put clothes or sheets in this when you want to wash them. w ....
....

5 You use this to keep your food cold. Ours was made in Italy. f ....

6 Food is fried or boiled on this or you can roast food in it.
c ....

2 When do we use *of*, *by* and *in* after *make*?
Match the sentences (1–3) with answers (a–c).

1 My phone case is made of leather.
2 It was made by my grandfather.
3 It was made in his garage.

a to say the person or thing who does/did the action
b to say where it is/was made
c to describe the material

☼ Exam tip

The missing words are usually common grammar words. For example, the missing word could be a preposition like those in Exercise 2. Think carefully about each gap and decide what type of word is missing.

3 Match the words in the box to the correct category of words that are often missing in Part 5 tasks. An example for each is done for you.

| when | have | an | but | to | their | the |
| | will | ago | since | us | so | soon |

1 pronouns / personal adjectives: .....his.....
....
2 articles ....a......... ....
3 connecting words ......and...... ....
....
4 auxiliary verbs .....did..... ....
5 time words .....after..... ....
....

✓ Exam task

For each question, write the correct answer.
Write one word for each gap.

Example: **0** my

To: Lisa

I think I've lost **(0)** .... phone.
I **(1)** .... given it as a present just
(2) .... few weeks ago. I know I had it on Saturday before we went to the cinema with Jason. Have **(3)** .... seen it anywhere, Lisa? It's got a green case which says 'Made **(4)** .... Portugal' on it.

To: Baha

Don't worry! Theo **(5)** .... got it. He found it in his dad's car after they took us home. I'm going to meet Theo later. Shall I get the phone from him? Then I can bring it **(6)** .... we see each other tomorrow. Is that OK?

UNIT 1

1 Complete the dialogues with the correct form of *have got*.

1 **A:** .... (you) any brothers or sisters?
   B: Yes, I .... a sister and two brothers.
2 **A:** .... (Manuela) a sandwich for lunch?
   B: No, she .... She .... a salad.
3 **A:** .... (your parents) a car?
   B: No, ... but my mum .... a motorbike and my dad .... a bicycle!
4 **A:** It's raining. .... (you) an umbrella?
   B: No I ....
5 **A:** Daniel can't come swimming today because he .... any money.
   B: I .... some money so I can pay for him!

2 Write the correct word to finish the sentences.

1 My mother's mother is my ....
2 My mum and dad are my ....
3 My sister is my mother's ....
4 My uncle is my aunt's ....
5 My aunt's son is my ....
6 My mother is my father's ....
7 My uncle is my mum's ....
8 My mum and my uncle are my grandfather's ....

3 Choose the correct word to complete the sentences.

1 What time *do / does* you go to bed at the weekend?
2 Mariana *don't walk / doesn't walk* to school because it's too far.
3 Most students *go / goes* to the town centre on Saturday afternoons.
4 My brother *play / plays* football three times a week.
5 Where *do / does* your best friend live?
6 Linda *don't do / doesn't do* her homework at home – she goes to the library.
7 We *start / starts* school at eight am.
8 Do your friends *watch / watches* TV in the evening?

4 Choose the correct adjective to complete the sentences.

curly	dark	long	short	straight	tall

1 My dad's got black hair and mine is the same – it's very ....
2 My brother is very .... – he's almost 1.9 m.
3 I want to cut my hair because it's too ....
4 My sister's got very straight hair but mine is different – it's ....
5 Alison cut her hair last week. Now it's very ....
6 His hair is short, blond and .... It's not curly.

/27

UNIT 2

1 Rewrite these sentences with the word in brackets.

1 My mum takes photos of us. (often)

....

2 My best friend draws pictures of animals at art club. (usually)

....

3 I'm late for my music classes. (sometimes)

....

4 I go to the cinema with my cousins. (twice a month)

....

5 My friends do after-school activities. (every day)

....

6 We sleep in a tent in winter. (never)

....

2 Complete the gaps with *like* or *would like* and the correct form of the verb in brackets.

1 **A:** Where .... (you / go) for your next holiday?
   B: I .... (go) to the sea because I .... (swim).

2 **A:** What type of music .... (you / listen) to in your free time?
   B: I .... (listen) to rock and rap.

3 **A:** .... (you / come) to my birthday party next Saturday evening?
   B: Yes, thank you! I .... (go) to parties. What time does it start?

4 **A:** Which film .... (you / watch) at the cinema tonight?
   B: I .... (watch) the adventure film.

5 **A:** What .... (you / do) in your free time?
   B: I .... (play) the piano.

6 **A:** .... (you / eat) in restaurants or at home?
   B: I usually eat at home but I .... (go) to a restaurant sometimes.

3 Complete the sentences with a word or phrase from the box.

> cooking   dancing   going to concerts   messaging friends   playing computer games
> reading books   spending time with friends   trying new food

1 My brother is brilliant at .... He often makes dinner for the family.

2 I enjoy .... because I love seeing my favourite bands.

3 Irene hates going to discos because she is terrible at ....

4 My mum likes calling people on the phone but I prefer ....

5 I don't like .... in my free time because I have to read a lot for school.

6 When I go to a restaurant I'm always interested in ....

7 Jenny loves .... She always wins.

8 My sister doesn't like being alone. She prefers ....

/20

UNIT 3

1 Read the sentences and write the word.

1 We put all the plates, cups and glasses in this.   c....................
2 I look at this when I brush my hair.   m....................
3 If it's too dark, turn this on.   l....................
4 All my family sit on this and watch TV together.   s....................
5 I sit at this and do my homework.   d....................
6 At night, you lie down on this and go to sleep.   b....................
7 You have to put milk, cheese and meat in this.   f....................
8 To make a cake, fry an egg or boil vegetables, you need this. c....................

2 Choose the correct word to complete the sentences.

1 Let's buy *some / any* ice cream for the party.
2 There *is / are* two burgers and *some / any* potatoes on the table.
3 I'd like *a / an* salad for lunch.
4 There *is / are* a table and four chairs in the kitchen. We can eat there.
5 I don't want *some / any* meat.
6 Can I have *a / an* omelette?
7 Can you make *some / any* rice for lunch?
8 We haven't got *some / any* jam.

3 Complete the sentences with the correct form of *have to*.

1 I live near my school so I .... get up very early in the morning.
2 My mum says breakfast is very important so I .... have a big breakfast every day.
3 We .... wear a school uniform. It's grey and dark blue.
4 We go to school from Monday to Friday. We .... go to school on Saturday or Sunday.
5 .... (you) stay at school every afternoon until 4 p.m.?
6 I do homework every weekend but my sister .... do homework because she's only five years old.
7 After dinner I .... wash up and my sister sometimes helps me.
8 My sister .... go to bed at 8 p.m. but I usually go to bed at 9.30.

/24

UNIT 4

1 Write the *-ing* form of the verbs.

1 write ....
2 repair ....
3 decide ....
4 carry ....
5 listen ....
6 study ....
7 play ....
8 run ....

2 Complete these sentences with the words from the box.

| coat | costume | helmet | jeans | skirt | socks | T-shirt | trainers |

1 You can't wear those boots to go running. Put on your .... !
2 I want to go swimming. Where is my swimming .... ?
3 When you ride your bike, please put on your ....
4 You aren't wearing .... so your shoes are uncomfortable.
5 My sister doesn't like wearing trousers. She always wears a ....
6 We have to wear grey trousers at school. We can't wear ....
7 In the summer my brother and I usually wear a .... and shorts.
8 You have to wear your .... today because it's very cold outside.

3 Choose the present simple or the present continuous to complete these sentences.

1 Paul *does / 's doing* athletics in the park every Sunday.
2 Maths is really difficult for me. I *don't understand / 'm not understanding* it.
3 I *go / 'm going* fishing with my dad every Saturday afternoon.
4 Luis *does / is doing* his homework at the moment.
5 My best friend *comes / is coming* from Switzerland. She *speaks / is speaking* three languages.
6 How often *do you go / are you going* skiing?
7 Marianna *works / is working* hard for her exams because she *wants / is wanting* to go to university next year.
8 My football team *wins / is winning* the match!

4 Complete the sentences with the correct form of *play, do* or *go.*

1 In the winter, our class always .... ice-skating in the mountains.
2 We can .... table tennis at lunchtime in the school hall.
3 My sister .... volleyball in the school team. She's very good.
4 Do you .... athletics at school?
5 I .... skiing with my family every weekend.
6 I'd like .... surfing in the Atlantic Ocean.
7 My mum isn't here at the moment – she .... aerobics at the gym.
8 I sometimes .... cycling but I prefer .... skateboarding.

/32

Revision

UNIT 5

1 Write the past simple positive form of the verbs.

1 enjoy ....
2 visit ....
3 see ....
4 go ....
5 borrow ....
6 buy ....
7 play ....
8 arrive ....

2 Complete the names of the places in a town.

1 This is where you go to do different sports. s.................... c....................
2 We watch films here. c....................
3 A place where you can buy books. b....................
4 A shop where you can buy medicine. p....................
5 You can go here to read or borrow books. l....................
6 This is a big shop where you can buy lots of different things. d.................... s....................
7 People go here to watch plays. t....................
8 This is a place where adults study. u....................

3 Choose the correct words to complete the sentences.

1 My brother is three. He *was / were* born three *months / years* ago.
2 *Did / Were* you visit a museum on holiday?
3 I *didn't go / didn't went* shopping yesterday.
4 What *have you done / did you do* last weekend?
5 *Did / Was* the maths test easy?
6 Paul isn't here. He *leaved / left* ten *minutes / centuries* ago.
7 They *didn't liked / didn't like* the film.
8 Mariella *learned / did learn* to swim five years *ago / old*.

4 Complete the sentences with the past simple form of the verb in brackets and *at*, *on* or *in*.

1 I .... (be) born .... 3rd May 2005.
2 We .... (not play) football .... the weekend.
3 What .... you .... (do) .... the evening?
4 My friends .... (not be) at school .... 9 o'clock this morning.
5 The new cinema .... (open) in our town .... Saturday.
6 .... you .... (have) a good time .... your birthday?
7 My teacher .... (not work) at my school .... 2016.
8 My brother .... (begin) learning Chinese .... October.

/32

UNIT 6

1 Write the letters in the right order to spell the types of transport.

1 rehlcpeoti ....
2 ochca ....
3 rlyor ....
4 mtra ....
5 hpsi ....
6 btiomrkoe ....
7 xtai ....
8 abot ....

2 Complete the sentences with the comparative form of the adjective in brackets.

1 My brother is .... (old) than me.
2 A plane is .... (fast) than a car.
3 It's hot today but yesterday it was .... (hot).
4 My dad's new motorbike is .... (expensive) than a car.
5 I think English is .... (easy) than Chinese.
6 My house is .... (noisy) than the library so I go there to do my homework.
7 I can walk to school but my best friend lives .... (far) away than me so she goes by bus.
8 It is .... (healthy) to cycle to school than to take the bus.

3 Complete the sentences with the superlative form of the adjectives in brackets.

1 My favourite subject at school is science but it is also .... (difficult).
2 Julie is .... (quiet) student in the class. She never speaks.
3 The Roman bridge is .... (old) road bridge in our city.
4 It was .... (bad) holiday I've ever had!
5 The department store is always .... (crowded) shop in town.
6 We stayed at .... (cheap) hotel in town.

4 Choose the correct word to complete the sentences.

1 I often *ride / drive* my bike to school.
2 Yesterday we went to the cinema *by / on* foot.
3 We drove my aunt to Madrid airport and she took the *plane / tram* to New York.
4 I would love to *sail / fly* around the world in a small boat.
5 If you want to cross the road, use the *roundabout / crossing*.
6 My sister learnt to *drive / ride* a car last year.
7 We were late so we went to the theatre *by / on* taxi.
8 In my town, there are three *car parks / bridges* over the river.

/30

UNIT 7

1 Write the names of the school subjects next to the questions.

1 What's the past tense of the verb *eat*? ....
2 What is the name of the largest desert in the world? ....
3 When did Nelson Mandela die? ....
4 Which artist painted *Guernica*? ....
5 Which trees grow in the desert? ....
6 Can you play a musical instrument? ....
7 What is 12 plus 7? ....

2 Choose the correct verb to complete the sentences.

1 When I go to university I want to *teach / study* English.
2 Can you *learn / teach* me how to do the maths problems?
3 My sister *spends / uses* two hours every afternoon doing her homework.
4 If you *miss / lose* a class you should ask another student for the homework.
5 Alex is *passing / taking* his exam at the moment. He finishes at 11 a.m.
6 I go to music lessons after school because I want to *study / pass* my guitar exam.

3 Complete the sentences with the correct adverb from the box.

> badly   carefully   easily   quickly   quietly   well

1 Lucia can play the guitar very .... She's playing in the school concert.
2 Ethan passed the piano exam .... because he's very good at music.
3 The school football team is playing .... today so I don't think they will win the match.
4 We need to go .... The bus is leaving in five minutes.
5 Remember to check your spelling .... when you finish writing.
6 Can you speak .... please? I'm trying to study.

4 Choose the correct word to complete the sentences.

1 It's too dark in here. We *can't / mustn't* see anything.
2 You can't write your answers in pen. You *must / mustn't* write in pencil.
3 Shh! You *couldn't / mustn't* talk loudly in the library.
4 You *shouldn't / can't* worry so much about the exam.
5 My cousin is good at languages. She *can / could* speak English, French, Spanish and German.
6 My little brother had swimming lessons at school so he *can / can't* swim now.
7 I left my books at school so I *couldn't / mustn't* do my homework last night.
8 When my dad was young, he *could / should* play football very well.

/27

UNIT 8

1 Complete the sentences with a phrase from the box.

> explore the city   have a rest   learn a language   stay at a campsite
> stay with a family   stay at home   try new dishes

1 We went to Brazil for our last holiday. The journey was really tiring so when we got there we went to the hotel to ....
2 I wanted to have a cheap weekend break so I decided to borrow my friend's tent and
....
3 I'm going to Oxford for a language course. I want to .... so that I can practise my English.
4 I like to .... when I travel so I often visit local restaurants.
5 My brother isn't coming away with us. He has to .... to prepare for his exams next month.
6 I believe that the best way to .... is to go to the country where it is spoken.
7 We're going to Florence in Italy this summer because my parents want to ....

2 Complete the sentences with the correct form of the past continuous.

1 .... (your classmates / speak) English at 11 a.m. yesterday?
2 .... (I / have) a rest at 3 p.m. on Sunday.
3 .... (you / talk) when the class started?
4 .... (Carla / not sleep) last night at 11 p.m. She ....
(watch) TV.
5 .... (my dad / make) breakfast when I woke up this morning.
6 .... (it / not rain) when she left home this morning. It was sunny.
7 .... (you / have) lunch at 2 p.m. yesterday?
8 .... (my mum / read) a book when I went to bed last night.

3 Choose the correct adjective to complete the sentences.

1 I had a *terrible / brilliant* time at the concert. All my friends were there and we heard our favourite songs.
2 We went to the cinema last weekend. The film was so *funny / tiring* we laughed a lot.
3 The students were *bored / boring* during the long coach journey because there was no wifi.
4 The flight from London to Los Angeles took 15 hours – it was very *brilliant / tiring*.
5 We built a fire at the campsite. It was really *exciting / boring* to learn to do something new.

4 Choose the past simple or the past continuous form of the verbs to complete the text.

Yesterday I **(1)** *rode / was riding* my bike in the park when I **(2)** *saw / was seeing* a small cat. I **(3)** *wanted / was wanting* to take it home with me but it **(4)** *ran / was running* away when it **(5)** *saw / was seeing* me. When I **(6)** *arrived / was arriving* home my mum **(7)** *told / was telling* me that her friend **(8)** *looked / was looking* for her lost cat, so I **(9)** *told / was telling* her to go to the park quickly!

/29

UNIT 9

1 Complete these conversations. Use *be going to* and the verb in brackets.

1 **A:** We .... (go) to the circus. Would you like to come?
   B: .... (you / ask) Pippa to come, too?
2 **A:** I .... (play) football on Friday afternoon. What about you?
   B: I .... (not do) anything. I'm tired.
3 **A:** My brother .... (play) in a concert. Why don't you come and watch?
   B: Cool! .... (he / play) the piano?
4 **A:** We .... (watch) a DVD at Jake's house on Saturday afternoon. Are you free?
   B: No, sorry, I .... (study) for my history test.
5 **A:** .... (you / take) an umbrella?
   B: No! It .... (not rain) today.
6 **A:** .... (you / come) to the exhibition with us after school?
   B: I'm sorry I can't. I .... (do) my homework.

2 Choose the correct form of the verb to complete the sentences.

1 I'd love *to visit / visiting* my cousin at her home in Washington DC.
2 Our teacher wanted *to take / taking* us to the Art exhibition next week but it's closed.
3 I like both of the dresses. It's difficult *to choose / choosing* which one to buy.
4 I'm going to go to the mountains next weekend because I really enjoy *to climb / climbing*.
5 My sister said it was easy *to pass / passing* the English exam but I don't think that's true.
6 Andrea's hoping *to be / being* a musician when she's older.
7 The school has a theatre club but I'm not interested in *to learn / learning* about acting.
8 Do you mind *to see / seeing* a cartoon or would you prefer to see a film?

3 Complete the sentences with a word or phrase from the box.

music programme   play   quiz show   sports programme
the news   the weather

1 My favourite .... is on TV at 8 p.m. every Wednesday. I love trying to answer the questions.
2 We're going to see that new .... at the theatre in town. Do you want to come?
3 My grandmother watches .... every morning on TV, but she never goes out so I don't understand why she watches.
4 Last night I saw an excellent .... about my favourite band. They played all their best songs.
5 My mum and dad say it's important to watch .... so that you know what is happening in the world.
6 I love watching the .... in the evening. The journalist usually talks to football or tennis players.

4 Complete the sentences with the correct form of the words in *italics*.

1 My brother *sings* in a band. He's a brilliant ....
2 My cousin *acts* in plays in New York. He's a famous ....
3 I don't like *dancing* because I'm a terrible ....
4 You're very good at *art*. You should be an ....
5 Our teacher enjoys taking *photos*. He's a good ....
6 My best friend can't play the *drums* well. He isn't a good ....
7 I'm interested in *music*. I'd like to be a .... when I'm older.
8 Sophia loves *writing* stories. She's hoping to be a famous ....

/28

UNIT 10

1 Choose the correct words to complete the sentences.

1 Don't worry. We *won't / may* be late. It's only five o'clock.
2 I'm not sure but we *may / will* go to Portugal in the spring.
3 Put on warm clothes. It *will / won't* be cold outside. It's snowing.
4 There are some clouds in the sky. It *won't / may* rain later.
5 Let's play tennis now. It *won't / will* be dark later.
6 I'm certain you *will / may* win the race. You're the fastest runner.
7 It's very windy. Be careful – you *may / won't* lose your hat!

2 Complete these sentences with a words from the box.

> field   gate   hill   path   river   spring   wood

1 There are a lot of very old trees in the .... near our village.
2 Which is the longest ....? Is it the Nile or the Amazon?
3 The farmer has one .... for cows and another for sheep.
4 We often go for a walk along the .... by the lake.
5 My favourite times of year are .... and autumn.
6 If you walk to the top of the .... you can see for 10 kilometres.
7 We opened a big .... at the entrance to the farm.

3 Read the definitions and write the words.

1 Very bad weather.   s....................
2 Water which becomes hard because it is very cold.   i....................
3 Water from the clouds.   r....................
4 You need this to fly a kite.   w....................
5 It is dark and cold without this.   s....................
6 It is difficult to see with this weather.   f....................
7 Soft, white pieces of ice.   s....................

4 Complete the sentences with the correct form of the verbs in brackets.

1 We .... (be) late if we .... (not leave) now.
2 If it .... (rain) tomorrow I .... (not go) to the beach.
3 What .... (you / do) if you .... (not pass) the exam?
4 Our teacher .... (get) angry if we .... (not remember) to do our homework.
5 If we .... (go) to the mountains at the weekend .... (you / come) with us?
6 If you .... (not go) to bed now you .... (be) tired tomorrow.
7 Marc .... (be) sad if you .... (not come) to his birthday party.
8 If you .... (miss) the bus how .... (you / get) to school?

/29

UNIT 11

1 Choose the correct word to complete the sentences.

1 I've broken my *arm / leg* so I can't write for two weeks.
2 She had a green and blue scarf around her *hand / neck*.
3 The girl held a biscuit in her *hand / foot*.
4 Her *foot / tooth* hurts so she's going to the dentist's in the town centre.
5 Dad had to lie down because he had a pain in his *back / hair*.
6 That photo is very dark. I can't see your *back / face*.
7 Caroline cut Joanna's *hair / hand* – it looked great.

2 Complete the sentences with the present perfect form of the verbs in brackets.

1 I .... (pass) my maths exam! I'm really happy.
2 I .... (never go) to Paris but I would like to go there next year.
3 Paul .... (fall) off his bike. Let's help him.
4 How long .... (you / know) your best friend?
5 My parents .... (not / decide) which film to see on Saturday evening.
6 I love watching tennis but I .... (not play) it before.
7 Eddie .... (not finish) his homework so he can't come to my house.
8 .... (you / eat) dinner yet? I want to go to the new Chinese restaurant.

3 Choose the correct words to complete the sentences.

Hi Lianne,
I'm so sorry that I haven't answered your message but I've been really busy studying for my exams.
Have you finished your exams **(1)** *just / yet*? I'm really excited that you're coming to stay with me.
I haven't seen you **(2)** *for / since* your birthday last year. Have you bought your train ticket **(3)** *just / yet*?
My mum has **(4)** *just / yet* booked tickets for the Healthy Body exhibition but we haven't decided where
to eat afterwards **(5)** *already / yet*. I haven't been to the Italian restaurant **(6)** *for / since* a month so I'd like
to go there.
Anyway, I have to go because it's **(7)** *already / yet* 6 o'clock and I haven't done my homework **(8)** *just / yet*.
Best wishes,
Alicia

4 Complete the sentences with the correct adjective from the box.

| angry | happy | hot | hungry | sick | sorry | thirsty | tired |

1 Can I have a drink please? I'm really ....
2 The boys went to bed very late last night so today they are ....
3 I'm .... I'm late. There was a lot of traffic.
4 It's .... today. Why don't we go swimming?
5 I don't want a sandwich because I'm not very ....
6 Alina had to go to the doctor's yesterday because she was feeling ....
7 My mum was really .... because I arrived home late.
8 Chris was so .... to see his friend Marcus after such a long time.

/31

UNIT 12

1 Write complete sentences in the present passive.

1 My shoes / made of leather.

....

2 I / give money for my birthday.

....

3 Rugby / not play at my school.

....

4 English / speak all over the world.

....

5 CDs / not sell here anymore.

....

6 My brother / call Kieran

....

2 Complete the sentences with the past passive form of the verbs.

1 My new phone .... (make) in Japan.
2 This book .... (write) by my cousin.
3 This record player .... (use) by my dad when he was a child.
4 The tennis match .... (won) by my best friend.
5 My brother .... (teach) English by our aunt.
6 The students .... (give) extra homework by the maths teacher.

3 Complete the sentences with the words in the box.

| address | alarm | download | mobile | online | play | send | use |

1 At school we can't .... the internet because the wifi is broken.
2 I prefer to call my friends but my brother prefers to .... messages.
3 Would you like to come to my house to .... computer games on Saturday?
4 I've asked my parents for a new .... phone for my birthday.
5 The teacher gave us her email .... so that we could send her the homework.
6 We were told not to .... films or music from the internet.
7 I am always late for school so my mum bought me a new .... clock.
8 Do you often post messages .... ?

4 Choose the correct word to complete the sentences.

1 It's important to keep milk in the *cooker / fridge*.
2 Our *washing machine / cooker* broke last week so we didn't have any clean clothes.
3 I have a *lamp / clock* next to my bed because I like reading before I go to sleep.
4 My best friend gave me a new *case / mouse* for my phone – it's gold.
5 If the *screen / keyboard* on your phone is dirty, how can you clean it?
6 I sometimes take my *internet / laptop* to school with me.

/26

Grammar reference

UNIT 1

have got and present simple

have got

Have got and *have* mean the same thing. *Have got* is more informal.

Positive / Negative forms		
I / You / We / They	**have / 've got**	a digital camera.
	haven't got	
He / She / It	**has / 's got**	
	hasn't got	

Question forms		
Have	I / you / we / they	**got** a digital camera?
Has	he / she / it	

Short answers		
Yes,	I / you / we / they	**have**.
	he / she / it	**has**.
No,	I / you / we / they	**haven't**.
	he / she / it	**hasn't**.

In short answers we do not use *got*.
✓ *Yes, I* **have**.
✗ *Yes, I have got.*

Use *have got* to talk about:
• things we own:
I've got a new mobile.
He's got an unusual name.

• how people look:
She's got blue eyes.
Tom's got brown hair.

• our family and friends:
I've got two brothers and a sister.
My mum's got two cousins.

Practice

1 Choose the correct words to complete the sentences.

1 Lauren *hasn't / haven't* got any shoes to wear for the party.
2 Alex and Liza *has / have* got two cousins each.
3 My brother and I *has / have* got black hair.
4 **A:** *Has / Have* we got any homework tonight?
   B: No, we *hasn't / haven't*.
5 All my friends *has / have* got mobile phones.

2 Complete these sentences with the correct form of *have got*.

1 My family is very big. I.......................................three brothers and two sisters.
2 She can't go skateboarding because she ....a skateboard.
3 My older brother Ben ....a new car.
4 **A:** I don't know where my scarf is. ....you ....it?
   B: No, I.......................................
5 I'm sorry, but we ....any coffee.

Present simple

be

Positive / Negative forms		
I	**am / 'm**	13 years old. Spanish. happy.
	am not / 'm not	
You / We / They	**are / 're**	
	are not / aren't	
He / She / It	**is / 's**	
	is not / isn't	

Question forms		
Am	I	13 years old? Spanish? happy?
Are	you / we / they	
Is	he / she / it	

Short answers		
Yes,	I **am**.	
	you / we / they **are**.	
	he / she / it **is**.	
No,	I**'m not**.	
	you / we / they**'re not**.	
	you / we / they **aren't**.	
	he / she / it**'s not**.	
	he / she / it **isn't**.	

We use *be* to talk about:
• nationality: *I'm French.*
• age: *She's 14.*
• jobs: *My mum and dad* **are** *teachers.*
• feelings: ***Are*** *you happy?*
• time: *It's ten o'clock.*
• where things are: *The plates* **are** *on the table.*

Practice

Read the sentences and rewrite the short forms of the underlined words.

1 <u>You are</u> 16 years old. ..You're..........
2 My brother <u>is not</u> very funny. ....
3 **A:** Are you Spanish?
  B: No, <u>I am not</u>. ....
4 We <u>are not</u> teachers. ....
5 We <u>are</u> students. ....
6 <u>She is</u> Australian. ....

Complete the sentences with the correct form of *be*.

1 My sister .... 19.
2 I .... not very happy this morning.
3 Two of my friends .... American.
4 **A:** .... your mother a doctor?
  B: No, she .... She .... an engineer.
5 **A:** .... you 12 years old?
  B: Yes, I ....

Other verbs in the present simple

Positive / Negative forms

I / You / We / They	**like**	chocolate.
	don't like	
He / She / It	**likes**	
	doesn't like	

Question forms

Do	I / you / we / they	**like** chocolate?
Does	he / she / it	

Short answers

Yes,	I / you / we / they	**do**.
	he / she / it	**does**.
No,	I / you / we / they	**don't**.
	he / she / it	**doesn't**.

The *he / she / it* form of most verbs uses the infinitive + -*s*. Sometimes we add -*es* (*do → does; go → goes*). If the verb ends in consonant -*y*, we replace -*y* with (*carry → carries*).

We use present simple verbs to talk about:
- things that happen regularly: *We **go** to school every weekday.*
- things or facts that are always true:
*Summer **comes** after spring.*
- things that are generally true and are true now:
*We **live** in Paris.*
- with verbs that describe states (things that don't change), e.g.: *be, like, hate, have, want, love, know, understand*:
*I **like** apples but I **hate** oranges.*
*I **have** three cousins, and I **love** them all.*

Practice

1 Complete the sentences with the present simple form of the verbs in brackets.

1 Lucas .... (play) the piano every evening.
2 I .... (get up) at nine o'clock at the weekend.
3 My brother .... (like) football.
4 My friends .... (live) near me.
5 Hannah .... (go) to school by bus.

2 Write the negative form of the sentences in Exercise 1.

1 Lucas ....
2 I ....
3 My brother ....
4 My friends ....
5 Hannah ....

3 Write questions and short answers.

1 you / go / school / on Saturdays?
  Do you go to school on Saturdays? Yes, I do. / No, I don't.
2 your mum / get home / at 4 p.m. / every day?
  ....
3 they / walk / to school / on Tuesdays?
  ....
4 he / start school / at 8.45?
  ....
5 you / have / breakfast / every day?
  ....

4 Underline and correct the mistakes in these sentences.

1 My father work in London.
2 Tom don't play an instrument.
3 I plays tennis every weekend.
4 Does she starts work at nine o'clock every morning?
5 My parents doesn't watch TV in the afternoon.

Question words

Here are some of the most common question words we use to ask about:

• time: **What time** do you go to school? At eight o'clock.
• a time, day or date: **When** do you meet your friends in town? On Saturdays.
• a place: **Where** do you play tennis? At the sports centre.
• a thing: **What** is your favourite colour? Green.
• the way we do something: **How** do you go into town? By bus.
• a person: **Who** do you go shopping with? My dad.

1 Complete the questions with the correct question word.

1 .... is Sophia? She's at the dentist.
2 .... do you have lunch? At 12.30.
3 .... does George watch TV? In the evening.
4 .... do they get to school? They walk.
5 .... do you have for breakfast? Cereal and toast.
6 .... do you talk to online? My friends.

UNIT 2

Adverbs of frequency, *Do you like ... ? / Would you like ... ?*

Adverbs of frequency

Adverbs of frequency tell us how often something happens.

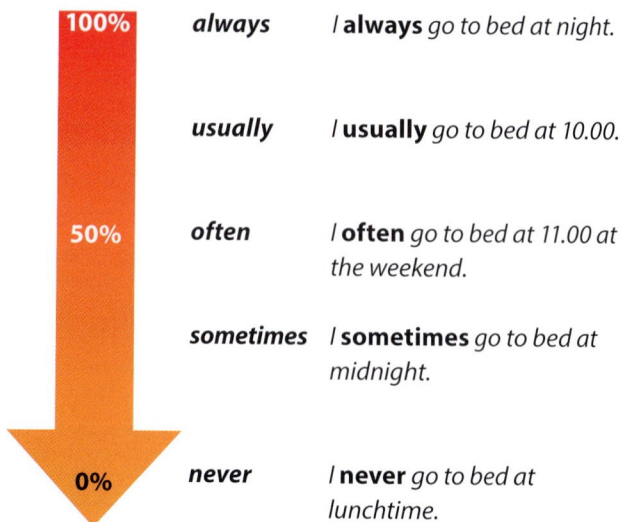

100%	always	I **always** go to bed at night.
	usually	I **usually** go to bed at 10.00.
50%	often	I **often** go to bed at 11.00 at the weekend.
	sometimes	I **sometimes** go to bed at midnight.
0%	never	I **never** go to bed at lunchtime.

We use adverbs of frequency after the verb *be*:
They **are always** happy at the weekend.
We usually put adverbs of frequency before all other verbs:
I **often get** home at five o'clock.
In negative sentences, frequency adverbs come between the negative form of the auxiliary verb (e.g. *be*, *do* and *have*, etc.) and the main verb:
We **don't always get up** early at the weekend.
We can also use phrases like *every day, twice a week, once a year* to say how often something happens. We usually put these at the end of the sentence:
We go on holiday to Italy **every year**.
I have guitar lessons **once a week**.

Practice

1 Put the words in order to make sentences.

1 evening. / go / I / in / never / school / the / to
2 help / homework. / me / My / my / parents / sometimes / with
3 and / I / brother / day. / every / My / school / to / walk
4 am / for / I / late / school. / sometimes
5 always / at / hard / I / school. / work

2 Make these sentences true for you. Use adverbs of frequenc

1 get up at seven o'clock in the morning
....
2 have lunch at school
....
3 go out in the evening
....
4 go to bed at ten o'clock
....
5 sleep eight hours a day
....

Do you like ... ? / Would you like ... ?

We use *Do you like* + *-ing* form of the verb + *?* to ask someone about their likes and dislikes:
Do you like doing homework?
Yes, I do. / No, I don't.

We usually use *I like / love / hate / enjoy / prefer* + *-ing* form of the verb to talk about these likes and dislikes:
I **enjoy reading**, but I **prefer watching** films.

We can use *Would you like* + *to* + infinitive + *?* to invite someone to do something. We can answer this invitation with, for example, *Yes, please! I'd love to. / No, thanks! I'm afraid I'm busy.*
Would you like to join the Theatre Club?
Yes, please. I'd love to.

Practice

1 Choose the correct words to complete the sentences.

1 *Would / Do* your parents like cooking?
2 **A:** There's a new action film on at the cinema.
   Would / Do you like *to come / coming*?
   B: Yes, please. I *love / hate* going to the cinema.
3 *Would / Do* you like drawing?
4 *Would / Does* your brother like to bake a cake?
5 **A:** *Would / Do* you and your friends like to watch a film?
   B: I'm afraid we *can't / can*. We need to study.
6 *Would / Do* you like playing football?

UNIT 3

There is / are, a / an, some & any, (don't) have to

There is / are

We use *there is* with singular countable nouns and uncountable nouns:
Remember! Countable nouns are things we can count.
Uncountable nouns are things we can't count.
There's a lamp on the table. (*lamp* = countable)
There's milk in the fridge. (*milk* = uncountable)

We use *there are* with plural countable nouns:
There are eggs in the fridge.

a / an

We use *a* and *an* before a singular countable noun: **a** burger,
an onion

some / any & a / an

We use *some* with plural countable nouns and with uncountable nouns in positive sentences:
There are **some** potatoes. (*potatoes* = countable)
There's **some** rice. (*rice* = uncountable)

We use *some* in offers and requests:
Would you like **some** dessert?
Can I have **some** jam, please?

We use *any* with plural countable nouns and uncountable nouns in negative sentences and questions:
Are there **any** vegetables?
No, there aren't **any** vegetables.

Is there **any** cheese?
No, there isn't **any** cheese.

Practice

1 Complete the sentences with *there is / are, a / an, some* or *any*.

1 Would you like .... apple?
2 .... six chairs in the kitchen.
3 Do we need .... vegetables?
4 .... students are not at school today.
5 Please, can I have .... water?
6 We haven't got .... homework.
7 .... a mobile phone on the floor.
8 .... there any books on the bookshelf?

(don't) have to

We use *have / has to* + infinitive to talk about things that are necessary:
We **have to go** to school five days a week.

We use *don't have / doesn't have to* + infinitive to talk about things that are not necessary:
We **don't have to go** to school at the weekend.

Positive / Negative forms		
I / You / We / They	**have to**	go to school tomorrow.
	don't have to	
He / She / It	**has to**	
	doesn't have to	

Question forms		
Do	I / you / we / they	**have to** go to school tomorrow?
Does	he / she / it	

Short answers		
Yes,	I / you / we / they	**do.**
	he / she / it	**does.**
No,	I / you / we / they	**don't.**
	he / she / it	**doesn't.**

Practice

1 Complete the conversation with the correct form of *have to* and the verbs in brackets.

A: Hi. Do you want to go swimming?
B: No, I can't. My sister and I **(1)** ....
(help) our parents.
A: What **(2)** .... (you do)?
B: To start with, I **(3)** .... (tidy) my bedroom.
A: And your sister? **(4)** .... (tidy) her bedroom, too?

B: Yes, (5) ...., and then we
(6) .... (do) the washing-up.
And you?

A: I (7) .... (not do) anything!

2 Choose the correct form of *have to* complete the sentences.

1 Teachers *have to / don't have to* work in schools.
2 Students *have to / don't have to* go to school in the holidays.
3 Young children *have to / don't have to* go to work.
4 Farmers *have to / don't have to* work outdoors.
5 Most police officers *have to / don't have to* wear uniforms.

UNIT 4

Present continuous

Positive / Negative forms		
I	am / 'm	
	am not / 'm not	
You / We / They	are / 're	
	are not / aren't / 're not	eating.
He / She / It	is / 's	
	is not / isn't / 's not	

Question forms		
Am	I	
Are	you / we / they	eating?
Is	he / she / it	

Short answers		
Yes,	I **am**.	
	you / we / they **are**.	
	he / she / it **is**.	
No,	I**'m not**.	
	you / we / they **'re not**.	
	you / we / they **aren't**.	
	he / she / it**'s not**.	
	he / she / it **isn't**.	

We can use the present continuous verbs to talk about things that are happening now:
I'm watching a film on TV.

Spelling of present continuous verbs		
Most verbs	add -*ing* to the infinitive	*watch* → **watching** *find* → **finding**
Verbs ending in -*e*	take off -*e*, then add -*ing*	*like* → **liking** *write* → **writing**
Verbs ending in vowel + consonant (with stress on last syllable)	repeat the last consonant and add -*ing*	*put* → **putting** *run* → **running**
Verbs which end in a vowel + -*l*,	double the -*l* and add -*ing*	*travel* → **travelling**

Practice

1 Complete the sentences with the present continuous form of the verbs in brackets.

1 My parents .... (not watch) TV.
They .... (listen) to music.
2 I .... (write) an email to my cousin in France.
3 **A:** .... (you / do) your homework?
B: No, I .... (not). I
.... (play) a computer game.
4 Tom .... (run) to school because he's late.
5 Maria .... (not wash) her hair.

2 Underline and correct the mistakes in the sentences.

1 Ben is readding one of his school books.
2 Emma and Anna are puting their clothes away.
3 Are you cookeing our lunch?
4 I'm siting in the kitchen.
5 My brother and sister are danceing in the garden.

Present continuous vs present simple

We use the present continuous to talk about things that are happening now:
We're watching television at the moment.

We use the present simple:
• to talk about things we do regularly:
I usually watch television in the evening.
I walk to school every day.

• to talk about things or facts that are always true:
Winter comes after autumn.

• to talk about things that are generally true and are true now:
We live in Zaragoza.

• with verbs that describe states (things that don't change), e.g. *be, like, hate, have, want, love, know, understand:*

*I **like** tea but I **hate** coffee.*
*I **have** three brothers, and I **love** them all.*

We do not usually use state verbs in the present continuous:
*I **understand** German and Spanish.*
~~*I am understanding German and Spanish.*~~

The verb *have* can be either a state verb or an action verb, but it has a different meaning:
*I **have** two brothers. (have = to own, state verb)*
*We're **having** breakfast. (have = to eat, action verb)*

Practice

1 Choose the correct verb to complete the sentences.

1 My brother and I *go / are going* to school by bus every day.
2 Dan can't come out. He *does / is doing* his homework.
3 I *love / am loving* school holidays.
4 Oh, no! It *starts / 's starting* to rain.
5 My sister and I *play / are playing* tennis every Saturday.
6 In our family, we *have / are having* a dog and three cats.

2 <u>Underline</u> and correct the mistakes in these sentences.

1 After school, we are usually getting home at five o'clock.
2 Be quiet! I listen to the news.
3 Everyone in my family is hating cold weather.
4 Ben is having a brother and a sister.
5 Jon has a shower at the moment.
6 Am I speaking too quickly? Do you understanding me?

UNIT 5

Past simple

be

Positive / Negative forms		
I / He / She / It	**was** **wasn't**	at home yesterday.
You / We / They	**were** **weren't**	

Question forms		
Was	I / he / she / it	at home yesterday?
Were	you / we / they	

Short answers		
Yes,	I / he / she / it	**was**.
	you / we / they	**were**.
No,	I / he / she / it	**wasn't**.
	you / we / they	**weren't**.

We use *was / were* to talk about the past:
*We **were** at school yesterday. Our new teacher **wasn't** very interesting.*
***Was** the film good? Yes, it **was**.*

Other verbs

Positive / Negative forms		
I / You / We / They / He / She / It	**enjoyed** **didn't enjoy**	the film last night.
	saw **didn't see**	

Questions forms		
Did	I / you / we / they / he / she / it	**enjoy** the film?
		see the film?

Short answers		
Yes,	I / you / we / they / he / she / it	**did**.
No,		**didn't**.

We use the past simple to talk about events / actions / states in the past which have finished:
*We **studied** a lot today.*
*They **lived** in Rome for five years.*

We often use time expressions with past simple verbs, for example, *last year, yesterday, on Tuesday, at 10 pm,* etc.

ago & the past simple

We also use *ago* to say how long it is since something happened. We normally use *ago* with the past simple. We put *ago* at the end of the sentence and after the time expression:
*I saw him a week **ago**.*
*She decided to become a doctor a long time **ago**.*

Spelling of regular past simple verbs		
Most verbs	add -ed	*watch* → **watched**
Verbs ending in -e	add -d	*like* → **liked**
Verbs ending in a consonant + -y	change -y to -i and add -ed	*study* → **studied**
Verbs ending in vowel + consonant (with stress on last syllable)	double the last consonant and add -ed	*stop* → **stopped**
Verbs ending in a vowel + -l	double the -l and add -ed	*travel* → **travelled**

Irregular verbs

There are many irregular past simple verbs in English (see pages 130–131):
*We **left** home at 8.30.*
*We **went** on holiday to France last year.*

Practice

1 Complete the short conversations with the past simple form of the verbs in brackets.

1 **A:** Why .... (be) you late for school yesterday?
   B: Our bus .... (break) down, so we .... (have to) walk.

2 **A:** What .... (do) you .... (have) for breakfast this morning?
   B: I .... (eat) toast and eggs and I .... (drink) orange juice.

3 **A:** What .... (do) you .... (get) for your birthday?
   B: I .... (get) a new phone from my parents and my sister .... (give) me a T-shirt.

4 **A:** .... (do) you .... (go) out yesterday?
   B: Yes, we .... (do) We .... (go) to town.

5 **A:** .... (do) you .... (watch) the football match on TV?
   B: No, I .... (do not). My dad .... (take) me to the game. It .... (be) great!

6 **A:** I .... (come) to see you this morning, but you .... (not be) in.
   B: Sorry, I .... (be) at the dentist.

2 Complete the sentences with the past simple form of the irregular verbs in the box.

begin	buy	feel	leave	make	meet	win

1 We .... home this morning at 7.30.

2 I .... two races at the weekend but I .... very tired afterwards.

3 My brother and I .... lunch for the whole family yesterday.

4 I .... my friends in town on Saturday. We .... some new clothes.

5 I .... to do my homework at seven o'clock. That was three hours ago.

Time expressions: *in / at / on*

We use *in*, *at* and *on* when we talk about time.

in	parts of the day	*I go to school **in the morning** and come home **in the evening**.*
	months, seasons	*My birthday is **in May**.* *We go on holiday **in summer**.*
	years	*I was born **in 2002** and started school **in 2007**.*
	other phrases	*I did my homework **in two hours**.*
at	clock times	*I get up **at six o'clock**.* *I have lunch **at midday**.*
	some festivals	*We have parties **at New Year**.*
	meal times	***At lunchtime**, we sometimes go to the café.*
	with *weekend* and *night*	*What do you do **at the weekend**?* *I often work **at night**.*
	other phrases	*I'm studying **at the moment**.*
on	days of the week	*I play football **on Saturdays**.* *Let's meet **on Monday evening**.*
	dates	*The match is **on 3rd April**.* *School starts on **4th September**.*

Practice

1 Complete the sentences with *in*, *at* or *on*.

1 We don't go to school .... Sundays.
2 I always go shopping .... the weekend.
3 Our holiday starts .... 23 December.
4 I do my homework .... the evening.
5 My sister's birthday is .... February.
6 I usually wake up .... seven o'clock.

2 <u>Underline</u> the mistakes in the sentences and correct them.

1 We often go swimming in Tuesday evenings.
2 We always have a big party on the end of the year.
3 My younger brother was born on 2013.
4 What do you eat in breakfast time?
5 Let's meet on the afternoon tomorrow.
6 I don't like working in night.

Comparative & superlative adjectives

We use comparative adjectives to talk about the difference between two people or things and to say who has more of something:

*I am **taller** than my best friend.*

*Hannah is **younger** than her sister.*

We use superlative adjectives to talk about the difference between three or more people or things and to say who has the most of something:

*I am **the tallest** student in my class.*

*Hannah is the **youngest** child in the family.*

We often use *than* after comparative adjectives: *I am **younger than** her.*
We often use *the* before superlative adjectives: *She is **the youngest** person in her family.*
We often use phrases like these after superlative adjectives: *in my family, in the world, in the class* (NOT ~~of the family, of the world, of the class~~).

Spelling of comparative and superlative adjectives		
Adjective	**Comparative**	**Superlative**
most adjectives, add *-er* or *-est*	**smaller, colder** than	the **smallest**, the **coldest**
adjectives ending in *-e* (e.g. *large, nice*), add *-r* or *-st*	**larger, nicer** than	the **largest**, the **nicest**
adjectives ending with a vowel + consonant (e.g. *big, thin*), double the consonant and add *-er* or *-est*	**bigger, thinner** than	the **biggest**, the **thinnest**
two-syllable adjectives ending in *-y* (e.g. *heavy, pretty*), change the *-y* to *-i* and add *-er* or *-est*	**heavier, prettier** than	the **heaviest**, the **prettiest**
some two-syllable adjectives add *-er*, *-est* or use *more, the most* These are adjectives ending in *-ow*, *-le*, *-er* and *polite*, *quiet*, *common* and *stupid*.	Sally is **more polite** than me. = Sally is **politer** than me.	Sally is **the most polite** girl in the class. = Sally is **the politest** girl in the class.
with two-syllable adjectives ending in *-ful* or longer adjectives (e.g. *difficult, important*), add *more* or *most*	**more difficult, more important** than	the **most difficult**, the **most important**
irregular adjectives (e.g. *good, bad, far*)	**better, worse, farther / further*** than	the **best**, the **worst**, the **farthest / furthest***

* *further / the furthest* are more common.

Practice

1 Complete the sentences with the comparative form of the adjectives in brackets.

1 My class is .... (big) than my brother's class.
2 Today's homework is .... (interesting) than yesterday's homework.
3 My new bike is .... (heavy) than my old one.
4 The sea is .... (warm) than it was last week.
5 The weather today is .... (bad) than it was yesterday.
6 These shoes are too small. I need .... (large) ones.

2 Choose the correct words to complete the sentences.

1 Jack is *the most / more* intelligent boy in the class.
2 Do you live in the *larger / largest* city in your country?
3 I am the *worst / more bad* runner in the team.
4 Julie is the *more happy / happiest* girl in the world today because it's her birthday.
5 He always takes the *biggest / bigger* piece of cake.
6 Is this Italian restaurant the *better / best* restaurant in town?

3 Underline the mistakes and correct them.

1 I am the better footballer in my class.
2 Anna is happyer than she was this morning.
3 I want to be fiter so I do lots of exercise.
4 What is the more expensive thing you own?
5 Ben's apartment is largerer than mine.
6 Tom is taller his father.

UNIT 7

Modals (*must / mustn't, should / shouldn't*)

must / mustn't

We use *must / mustn't* + infinitive without *to*:
• to talk about something that is important and where there is no choice:
*We **must be** at school by 8.30 every morning.*
*We **mustn't be** late.*

• to give advice that someone should follow:
*You **must be** careful when you cross the road.*
*You **mustn't cross** the road without looking.*

must does not change its form:

I / You / We / They / He / She / It	**must wear** a uniform for school.
	mustn't be late for school.

Practice

1 Complete the sentences with *must* or *mustn't* and verbs from the box.

be finish run talk use wear

1 Let's hurry. We .... late or we'll miss the start of the film.
2 You .... trainers when you play tennis.
3 You .... across the road. It's very dangerous.
4 Shh! You .... in the library!
5 Put your phone away. You .... it in the cinema.
6 I .... my homework by tomorrow.

2 Complete the advice to someone visiting your area. Use *must* or *mustn't* and a verb.

1 .... the museum. It's really interesting!
2 .... the taxis. They're very expensive. Use the tram instead.
3 .... the Italian restaurant. The food is fantastic.
4 .... your passport. Keep it somewhere safe!
5 .... the cathedral. It's a beautiful building.

should / shouldn't

We use *should / shouldn't* + infinitive without *to* to give someone advice.

*You **should do** more exercise.*
*You **shouldn't eat** too much before you go to bed.*

Positive / Negative forms

I / You / We / They / He / She / It	**should** eat more fruit and vegetables.
	shouldn't eat a lot of fast food.

Question forms and short answers

Should	I / you / we / they he / she / it	**ask** someone to help me?
Yes,	I / you / we / they he / she / it	**should**.
No,	I / you / we / they he / she / it	**shouldn't**.

Practice

1 Complete the table with the advice to students before an exam.

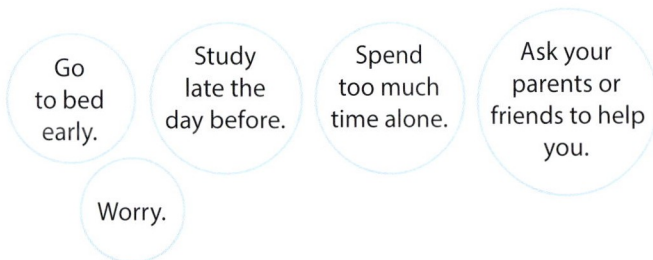

Go to bed early.

Study late the day before.

Spend too much time alone.

Ask your parents or friends to help you.

Worry.

You should …	You shouldn't …

2 Complete the sentences with *should* or *shouldn't* and the verbs in the box.

arrive   drink   eat   get   ride   wear

1 If it's very hot, you .... a lot of water.
2 If it's cold, you .... a coat.
3 You .... too much sugar. It's bad for your teeth.
4 You .... that bike. It's broken.
5 If you're always tired you .... more sleep.
6 Students .... late for classes.

can / could

Positive / Negative forms

I / You / We / They / He / She / It	**can / could** swim.
	can't / couldn't swim.

Question forms

Can **Could**	I / you / we / they / he / she / it	swim?

Short answers

Yes,	I / you / we / they / he / she / it	**can / could**.
No,		**can't / couldn't**.

We use *can / can't, could / couldn't* + infinitive without *to*. The forms of *can / can't* and *could / couldn't* don't change:
✓ I **can** cook.
X I **cans** cook.

We use *can / can't* to talk about present abilities (things that we are able to do now):
I **can play** the piano.
I **can't play** the guitar.
Can you speak French?
Yes, I **can**. / No, I **can't**.

We use *could / couldn't* to talk about past abilities (things that we were able to do in the past):
My sister **could talk** before she **could walk**.
I **couldn't sleep** last night.
Could you hear what I said?
Yes, I **could**. / No, I **couldn't**.

Practice

1 Complete these sentences with *can / can't* or *could / couldn't*.

1 I've broken my arm so I .... play tennis at the moment.
2 My best friend's mum is Spanish so my friend .... speak Spanish.
3 I .... hear what you're saying. The music is too loud.
4 My mother says I .... walk when I was one year old, but I .... when I was two.
5 **A:** .... you cook?
   B: No, I ....

2 Write questions starting with *can* or *could* and then give short answers that are true for you.

1 ride a bike when you were five?
A: Could you ride a bike when you were five?
B: Yes, I could.

2 swim when you were three?
....
....

3 speak more than two languages?
....
....

4 play basketball?
....
....

5 both of your parents drive?
....
....

Adverbs of manner

Adverbs of manner (*well, quickly, beautifully, etc.*) are used with verbs to describe how we do something:
*She's a good artist. She draws **well**.*
*He's a fast swimmer. He swims **fast**.*

We usually put the adverb after the verb + object:
*Sarah drove the car **carefully** down the road.*

Spelling of adverbs	
most adverbs, add -*ly* to the adjective	*quick → **quickly** slow → **slowly** beautiful → **beautifully***
adjectives ending in -*ble*, remove the -*e* and add -*y*	*comfortable → **comfortably***
adjectives ending in -*y*, remove the -*y* and add -*ily*	*easy → **easily***
adjectives ending in -*ic*, add -*ally*	*magic → **magically***
irregular adverbs	*good → **well** fast → **fast** hard → **hard** late → **late** early → **early***

Practice

1 Complete the sentences with the adverb form of the adjectives in the box.

beautiful	careful	comfortable	early	good	magic

1 You should wash your hands .... before you eat.
2 The rabbit appeared .... out of his hat.
3 You must always arrive .... before an exam.
4 Always dress .... when you go walking.
5 Did Julien do .... in the exam?
6 Charlotte sang .... at the concert.

UNIT 8

Past continuous

Positive / Negative forms			
I / He / She / It	**was**		**listening** to music.
	was not / wasn't		
You / We / They	**were**		
	were not / weren't		

Question forms		
Was	I / he / she / it	**listening** to music?
Were	you / we / they	

Short answers			
Yes,	I / he / she / it	**was.**	
	you / we / they	**were.**	
No,	I / he / she / it	**wasn't.**	
	you / we / they	**weren't.**	

We use the past continuous:
* to talk about something happening over a period of time in the past:
*We **were watching** a film at eight o'clock last night.*
* to talk about two things happening at the same time in the past:
*They **were watching** the film while I **was doing** my homework.*

Practice

1 Write sentences using the past continuous.

1 Jim / sleep / while / Sam / clean / the kitchen.
   Jim was sleeping while Sam was cleaning the kitchen.

2 What / you / do / last night / at ten o'clock?
   ....

3 It / be / not / rain / this morning.
   ....

4 I / have / a French lesson / while / they / have / an exam.
   ....

5 Sophie / be / not / travel / on the bus / at 8 a.m.
   ....

6 While / Jack / read / Emily / play / the guitar.
   ....

Past simple & past continuous

We use the past continuous with the past simple to talk about one thing happening in the middle of another:
*When I **left** home, my brother **was eating** his breakfast.*
*While I **was walking** into town, it **started** to rain.*

We use *when* with the past simple to talk about a point of time:
*My parents **were watching** TV **when** I **got** home.*

We use *while* with the past continuous to talk about the continuous actions:
*I **was doing** my homework **while** my parents **were watching** TV.*

Practice

1 Choose the correct verbs to complete the sentences.

1 I *slept / was sleeping* when you *phoned / were phoning* this morning.

2 At three o'clock this afternoon I *did / was doing* a maths test at school.

3 When I *woke up / was waking up* this morning, it *rained / was raining*.

4 What *are you doing / were you doing* at ten o'clock last night?

2 Complete the story with past forms of the verbs in the box. You need seven past continuous and two past simple verbs.

> be   come   ~~drive~~   listen   watch
> see   stand   tell   travel

It was a sunny morning and my parents, my sister and I **(1)** *were driving* .... along a busy motorway. We **(2)** .... to Scotland to spend the weekend with some friends. My sister and I **(3)** .... a film and Mum and Dad **(4)** .... to music. Suddenly, we **(5)** .... bright blue lights on the road in front of us. A policeman in a yellow jacket **(6)** .... in the middle of the road. He **(7)** .... everyone to drive more slowly. There were two fire engines at the side of the road near to a car. Smoke **(8)** .... out of its engine. Luckily, no one **(9)** .... hurt.

UNIT 9

be going to: positive & negative

Positive / Negative forms		
I	**am / 'm** **am not / 'm not**	
He / She / It	**is / 's** **is not / isn't**	**going to watch** TV all evening.
You / We / They	**are / 're** **are not / aren't**	

Question forms		
Am	I	
Is	he / she / it	**going to stay** in tonight?
Are	you / we / they	

Short answers		
Yes,	I	**am**.
	he / she / it	**is**.
	you / we / they	**are**.
No,	I	**'m not**.
	he / she / it	**'s not / isn't**.
	you / we / they	**aren't / 're not**.

We use *going to* + infinitive to talk about:
• future plans:
I'm going to spend all evening doing my homework.
I'm not going to fall asleep until I'm tired.
• things we predict because of something we can see or because of information we have now:

*My older sister **is going to have** a baby.*
*Look at those dark clouds. **It's going to rain**.*

Practice

1 Complete the sentences with *going to* and a verb from the box. There is one verb you do not need to use.

| do   miss   (not) need   ride   take   visit |

1 It's nearly eight o'clock. You
.... your bus.
2 Tomorrow morning we
.... our bikes to school.
3 I .... more exercise in future.
4 We .... our coats. It's sunny and warm outside.
5 My sister and I .... our grandparents at the weekend.

2 Complete the conversations with *going to*.

1 **A:** You / have coffee for breakfast?
Are you going to have coffee for breakfast?
B: No / tea.
No, I'm going to have tea.
2 **A:** What you / do this evening?
....
B: I / play a video game.
....
3 **A:** It / rain tomorrow?
....
B: No, it / sunny all day.
....
4 **A:** What you / do / when you leave school?
....
B: I / look / for a job in a sports centre.
....
5 **A:** your team / win / the match?
....
B: No, the other team is much better. We / lose.
....

Infinitives & *-ing* forms

We use *to* + infinitive after:		
some verbs	*choose, help, hope, learn, need, offer, want, decide*	I **hope to go** to university next year. He **wants to help** me. I'm **learning to speak** Italian.
adjectives	*happy, difficult*, etc.	They were **happy to see** me. This exercise isn't **difficult to do**. She was **surprised to hear** I was ill.
would like, etc.	*would like / (don't) like / enjoy / love / hate*	We**'d like to come** and see you later.

We use the *-ing* form after:		
some verbs	*enjoy, finish, mind, miss, keep*	I **enjoy watching** all sports. We **finished doing** our homework. I **miss seeing** my friends.
prepositions	*for, of, about*	Thanks **for helping** me.

Practice

1 Choose the correct verb forms to complete the sentences.

1 My dad offered *to help* / *helping* me with my homework.
2 I enjoy *to play* / *playing* the piano.
3 Let's finish *to watch* / *watching* the film before we go to bed.
4 My brother and I enjoy *to play* / *playing* video games.
5 Thank you for *to help* / *helping* me.

2 Underline the mistakes and correct them.

1 I hope visiting Brazil one day.
2 My friends and I always enjoy to meet in town on Saturdays.
3 I'm sorry hearing you're ill.
4 All my friends enjoy watch football.
5 Do you mind to wait a little longer?

UNIT 10

will / won't & may

will / won't

We can use *will / won't* + infinitive without *to* when we talk about the future.

Positive / Negative forms		
I / You / We / They / He / She / It	**will / 'll**	**see** you tomorrow.
	will not / won't	

Question forms		
Will	I / you / we / they / he / she / it	**see** Ben tomorrow?

Short answers		
Yes,	I / you / we / they / he / she / it	**will**.
No,		**won't**.

We use *will / won't*:
* to talk about things in the future:

I think **it will be** warm and sunny tomorrow.
I'm sure **it won't be** rainy and cold.

* to talk about things we decide to do at the time of speaking:

A: *The phone's ringing.*
B: *I'll answer it.*
A: *We haven't got any bread.*
B: *I'll go to the shop and buy some.*

We can use *will / won't*:
* to talk about things that may be possible in the future, often with these words and phrases:
* *think / don't think*:
  I **don't think** Brazil **will** win the match.

* *sure / certain*:
  I'm **sure** you**'ll pass** the English test.
  He's **certain** they **won't come**.

We often use *maybe*, *probably* and *perhaps* with *will*:
Maybe they**'ll** be late for the party.
I**'ll probably go** to bed quite late tonight.
Perhaps we**'ll have** a picnic at the weekend.

We can use *won't* to say something is impossible:
He **won't eat** a burger because he doesn't like fast food.

We can use *may* + infinitive when something is possible but not certain:
Jenny **may be** too busy to help us today.
It **may be** sunny tomorrow.

Practice

1 Ben asks six of his friends if they are coming to his party. Here are their replies. Who is going to the party?

1. I may come. I'll tell you tomorrow. (Suzie)
2. I'm not sure. I may have to check with my parents. (Hannah)
3. Yes, I'll be there. (Tom)
4. Probably not. I may have to go out with my parents. (Mike)
5. Of course I'll come. What time does it start? (Julie)
6. I hope so, but I may have to work. (Ryan)

2 Complete the sentences with *will*, *won't* or *may* and the verbs in brackets.

1. We .... (not have) time to go shopping before we leave. I'm not sure.
2. There's someone at the door. I .... (go) and see who it is.
3. **A:** .... you .... (be) away long?
   B: No, I ....
4. I .... (get) back home later tonight. It depends what time football practice finishes.
5. I probably .... (not pass) the maths test. I think it .... (be) really difficult.
6. I'm sure we .... (meet) again soon.

3 Put the words in order to make sentences.

1. for / go / holiday / next / our / Spain / to / We'll probably / year.
   ....
2. be / colder / I / it / think / tomorrow. / will
   ....
3. a / have / new / next / Perhaps / teacher / term. / we'll
   ....
4. Are / be / OK? / sure / you / you'll
   ....
5. come / He probably / our / party. / to / won't
   ....

First conditional

We use the first conditional to talk about likely situations / actions.

Conditional clause	Main clause (= future result)
if + present simple	*will / won't* + infinitive
If we **run**,	*we* **'ll catch** the bus.
If we **don't run**,	*we* **won't catch** the bus.

The conditional clause can start or finish the sentence:
If you **work** *hard, you* **'ll pass** *your exam.* (There is a comma after the conditional clause.)
You **'ll pass** *your exam if you* **work** *hard.* (There is no comma after the main clause.)
We can use the first conditional to talk about the future, but we use the present tense after *if*:
✓ *If you* **work** *hard, you* **'ll pass** *your exam.*
✗ *If you will work hard, you'll pass your exam.*

Practice

1 Complete the first conditional sentences with the correct form of the verbs in brackets.

1. If I .... (see) your best friend, I .... (tell) him to text you.
2. You .... (hurt) yourself if you .... (fall) over on the ice.
3. If we .... (not catch) the ten o'clock bus, we .... (have) to wait an hour for the next bus.
4. You .... (be) late to school if you .... (not leave) soon.
5. If the music .... (be) too loud, you .... (not hear) your phone.

2 Put the words in order to make first conditional sentences. Don't forget to add commas to some sentences.

1. earn / get / a holiday job / I / I'll / some money.
   If...
2. a bike / buy / enough money. / have / I / if
   I'll...
3. a / bike / to go / have / I / I'll / use / to school. / it
   If...
4. my bike / fit / get / I / if / ride / to school.
   I'll...
5. a bike / by bus. / don't have / enough / for / go / I / I'll / money / to school
   If...
6. by bus. / fit / get / go / I / if / to school
   I won't...

Present perfect

Positive / Negative forms		
I / You / We / They	have / 've have not / haven't	been to Australia. learned to cook.
He / She / It	has / 's has not / hasn't	

Question forms and short answers		
Have	I / you / we / they	been to Australia?
Has	he / she / it	
Yes,	I / you / we / they	have.
	he / she / it	has.
No,	I / you / we / they	haven't.
	he / she / it	hasn't.

The past participle form of regular verbs is the same as the past simple:

walk → **walked**

smile → **smiled**

You will need to learn the past participle form of irregular verbs*. Here are some common examples.

be	**been**
break	**broken**
come	**came**
do	**done**
eat	**eaten**
find	**found**
get	**got**
have	**had**
meet	**met**
see	**seen**
speak	**spoken**

* There is a list of irregular verbs on pages 130–131.

We can use the present perfect to talk about our experiences:

I**'ve seen** all the Harry Potter films, but I **haven't read** the books.

We do not use the present perfect to say when something happened:

✓ I**'ve been** to India.

✗ ~~I've been to India last year.~~

We use the past simple to say when something happened:

I **went** to India **last year**.

Present perfect: *just*

We use *just* to talk about something that happened a short time ago. We put *just* between *have / has* and the past participle.

I**'ve just spoken** to Paul.

My dad **has just got** home from work.

Present perfect: *yet*

yet (= *until now*) is used in negative sentences and questions to talk about things we plan to do in the future, but which are not done. *yet* is put at the end of a sentence:

Have you finished your homework **yet**?

I haven't read your email **yet.**

Present perfect: *already*

We use *already* to talk about something that happened before now or before we expected. We put *already* between *have / has* and the past participle:

I**'ve already had** my lunch. (I don't need to have lunch now.)

We**'ve already told** Mike where the match is. (Mike knows, so you don't need to tell him.)

Have you already finished your homework? That was quick! (The speaker did not expect this.)

We can also put *already* at the end of a sentence to show surprise or for emphasis:

Have you **downloaded** the music **already**?

Practice

1 Put the word in brackets in the correct position in these sentences.

1 Have you .... tidied your bedroom .... ? (yet)
2 They've .... finished .... their school project. (already)
3 I'm really hot. I've .... run home from school .... (just)
4 I don't want to watch that programme. I've .... seen it .... twice. (already)
5 Tania doesn't want .... to go to bed .... She isn't tired. (yet)

2 Put the words in order to make sentences.

1 I / haven't / my / new / shoes / worn / yet.

....

2 eating. / finished / just / We've

....

3 already / all / friends. / I've / my / texted

....

4 book / finished / Have / reading / that / yet? / you

....

5 brother. / I've / just / my / older / phoned

....

Present perfect with *for* & *since*

We can use the present perfect with *for* and *since* to talk about something that started in the past and is still happening in the present:

*I've known my best friend **for** a long time.* (= I knew my best friend in the past and I still know him now.)

*I've known her **since** 2012.* (= I met her in 2012 and I still know her now.)

for

We use the present perfect with *for* to talk about a period of time:
*I've studied English **for** six years.*
*We've lived in Berlin **for** three months.*

since

We use the present perfect with *since* to talk about when a situation started:
*I've studied English **since** 2015.* (I'm still studying it now.)
*We've lived in Berlin **since** June.* (We still live there.)

Practice

1 Complete the table with the time phrases in the box.

> 24 hours   six o'clock   400 years   last November   my birthday   October 12th   ten minutes   the end of May   three weeks   12 months   yesterday

For	Since

2 Choose the correct words or phrases in *italics*.

1 My sister's at university and I haven't seen her for *last weekend / two weeks*.
2 My parents have been married *for / since* 2000.
3 I haven't done any homework since *last week / one week*.
4 I've had my new bike since *yesterday / one day*.
5 My father has worked as a doctor *for / since* 23 years.
6 Juan has played the guitar since *the age of nine / nine years*.

The passive: present simple

We form the present simple passive by using the correct form of *be* followed by the past participle.

Active	Passive
They teach Russian at our school.	*Russian **is taught** at our school.*
We feed our cat twice a day.	*Our cat **is fed** twice a day.*

We use passive verbs rather than active verbs when:
• we don't know who does the action:
*Our school **is cleaned** every evening.*
(I don't know who cleans it.)
• we are more interested in who or what is affected by the action of the verb than who or what does the action:
*A lot of trainers **are made** in China.*
(Here the focus is on *trainers* rather than who makes them.)
*We **are** always **given** a lot of homework to do in the holidays.*
(Here *we* is the focus, not the homework, or the teachers who give the homework.)

To say who does something in the passive, we use *by* + the person or thing:
*English **is spoken by** most people in my country.*
*The TV show is very popular and **is watched by** three million people.*

Practice

1 Complete the sentences with the present simple passive form of the verbs in brackets.

1 A lot of tea .... (grow) in China.
2 Millions of bottles of water .... (sell) every day.
3 Interesting films .... (show) at the cinema in my town.
4 Our furniture .... (make) out of wood.
5 The road .... (close) today because of the storm.

The passive: past simple

We form the past simple passive by using *was / were* followed by the past participle.

Active	Passive
Someone stole my bike last week.	*My bike **was stolen** last week.*
They built our school in 2012.	*Our school **was built** in 2012.*

Practice

1 Complete the sentences with the past simple passive form of the verbs in the box.

build close give send take tell

1 Our house .... five years ago.
2 We .... how to get out if there is a fire in the building.
3 The shops .... all day Sunday.
4 I .... a watch for my birthday.
5 These photos .... on my phone.
6 I .... this email yesterday.

HOW TO MAKE YOUR WRITING BETTER: ADJECTIVES

To make a sentence more interesting, we can use adjectives.

1 Look at the pairs of sentences. <u>Underline</u> the adjectives in each b sentence.

1   a There was a chair in the corner of the room.
    b There was a <u>comfortable</u> chair in the corner of the room.

2   a We had lunch in a restaurant.
    b We had lunch in a small, friendly restaurant.

3   a A woman showed me the way home.
    b A kind woman showed me the way home.

4   a I knew I had made a mistake.
    b I knew I had made a big mistake.

2 Look at Exercise 1 again. Decide if the sentences are true or false.

Adjectives …

1   describe people or things.

2   usually come after the person or thing they describe.

3   can make sentences more interesting because they add more information.

3 Complete the sentences with an adjective from the box.

expensive   heavy   important   lovely   modern

1   He was carrying a .... suitcase.

2   I have an .... message for you.

3   She lives in a .... apartment.

4   We had a .... day in the park.

5   She was wearing an .... jacket.

4 We often use adjectives to talk about good or nice things. Choose the two adjectives which can replace *good* or *nice* in each sentence.

1   It was a very good film. (*exciting / friendly / funny*)

2   She was wearing a nice dress. (*beautiful / lovely / clever*)

3   That's a good idea. (*brilliant / famous / great*)

4   A nice doctor helped me. (*friendly / favourite / kind*)

5   The weather was nice. (*sunny / clever / pleasant*)

6   We had some good food. (*great / hungry / excellent*)

5 We often use adjectives to talk about very good or very bad things. <u>Underline</u> the adjectives which mean 'very good' or 'very bad' in each sentence. Then add them to the table.

1   It was a nice day. We had a <u>wonderful</u> meal.

2   We didn't play tennis because the weather was terrible.

3   I loved the film. It was amazing!

4   I didn't like the food. It was horrible.

5   We watched a film, but it was awful!

6   I think she's a fantastic singer. I love her songs.

very good	very bad
wonderful	

HOW TO MAKE YOUR WRITING BETTER: ADVERBS & INTERESTING VERBS

1 Look at the pairs of sentences. <u>Underline</u> the adverbs in each b sentence.

1 **a** I ran home.
   b I <u>quickly</u> ran home.

2 **a** The children were playing in the garden.
   b The children were playing happily in the garden.

3 **a** I read the invitation.
   b I read the invitation carefully.

4 **a** She opened the letter.
   b She opened the letter slowly.

5 **a** I couldn't see because it was cloudy.
   b I couldn't see well because it was cloudy.

2 Look at Exercise 1 again. Decide if the sentences below are true or false.

1 Adverbs can describe how someone does something.

2 Most adverbs end in -ly.

3 Adverbs always come before the verb.

4 Adverbs can make sentences more interesting, because they describe actions.

3 Choose the best adverb in each sentence.

1 A man called my name *loudly / terribly*.

2 The children ate their pizzas *kindly / hungrily*.

3 He spoke *clearly / cheaply*.

4 My mum was driving very *noisily / fast*.

5 She *carefully / busily* picked up the young bird.

6 We found the boat *easily / loudly*.

7 Everyone in the team played *quickly / well*, and we won the game!

8 She sang the song *beautifully / highly*.

4 Complete the sentences with the adverb in brackets. Choose the correct place to put the adverb.

1 The .... police officer spoke to me .... (angrily)
   The police officer spoke to me angrily.

2 I .... read the .... letter. (quickly)

3 She closed .... the door .... (quietly)

4 He .... carried the hot drinks into the sitting room .... (carefully)

5 We walked .... through .... the park. (slowly)

6 Mark didn't .... sleep .... last night. (well)

5 Sometimes we can use a more interesting verb instead of a verb and an adverb. <u>Underline</u> the verb in each b sentence which matches the verb + adverb in the first sentence.

1 **a** I <u>went</u> to the bus stop <u>quickly</u>.
   b I hurried to the bus stop.

2 **a** Everyone was <u>speaking loudly</u> at the same time.
   b Everyone was shouting at the same time.

3 **a** They were <u>sitting quietly</u> in the garden.
   b They were relaxing in the garden.

4 **a** We <u>got into</u> the water <u>quickly</u>.
   b We jumped into the water.

5 **a** I <u>put</u> the letter <u>quickly</u> into the bin.
   b I threw the letter into the bin.

6 **a** 'I'm lost,' she <u>said sadly</u>.
   b 'I'm lost,' she cried.

6 Complete the sentences with the verbs in the box.

jumped	ran	relaxed	shouted	threw

1 She .... into the room and picked up the phone.

2 'Go away!' he ....

3 We sat down and .... for a few minutes.

4 The girl .... onto her bike and rode away.

5 He .... the map onto the fire.

USE VERB FORMS CORRECTLY TO TALK ABOUT THE PAST, PRESENT & FUTURE

1 Read the email. <u>Underline</u> six mistakes with verb forms.

> ● ● ●
>
> Hi Jo,
>
> I go swimming next Saturday. My cousin are here at the moment, and he love swimming. Are you want to come too? There's a swimming pool on Wood Road. We can to get the bus. I meet you at the bus stop.
>
> Sam

2 Write the email from Exercise 1 correctly.

....
....
....
....

3 This email has more information. Read it and choose the correct verbs in *italics*.

> ● ● ●
>
> Hi Jo,
>
> I **(1)** *goes / 'm going / want go* swimming next Saturday. My cousin
> **(2)** *is / was / am* here at the moment and he **(3)** *is love / loves / loving* swimming.
> **(4)** *You want / Does you want / Do you want* to come too? There's a swimming pool
> on Wood Road. I **(5)** *never been / 've never been / never went* there, but Max **(6)** *went
> / has been / been* yesterday and he says it's great. We can **(7)** *get / getting / gets* the
> bus. I **(8)** *'m meeting / can to meet / can meet* you at the bus stop.

4 Look at Exercise 3 again. Find an example of these things.

1 the present continuous for future plans ....
2 the past simple for an action in the past ....
3 the present perfect for an experience at some time in the past ....
4 a modal verb ...., ...

5 Complete the email below with the correct form of the verbs in brackets.

> ● ● ●
>
> Hi Sara,
>
> I **(1)** .... (go) to a concert in Manchester next Saturday. My uncle
> **(2)** .... (buy) me two tickets for my birthday last month. The concert
> **(3)** .... (start) at eight o'clock. My friend Sam wants **(4)** ....
> (come) too. I think you **(5)** .... (meet) him a few times. We can
> **(6)** .... (go) for a pizza first if you want.

6 Use these notes to write an email. Try to use different verb forms correctly.

- ask a friend to come to a water park with you next Saturday
- say where it is
- say how you can get there

USE LINKING WORDS & RELATIVE PRONOUNS TO MAKE LONGER SENTENCES

1 Read the story. How many sentences are there?

> Dan woke up. He got out of bed. He didn't look at his clock. He opened the fridge. It was almost empty. He was hungry. He decided to go out for some food. He went to a café. It was closed. It was only 6.30 in the morning!

2 Read the same story. This time, the sentences are linked with linking words. <u>Underline</u> the linking words.

> Dan woke up <u>and</u> got out of bed. He didn't look at his clock. He opened the fridge, but it was almost empty. He was hungry, so he decided to go out for some food. He went to a cafe, but it was closed because it was only 6.30 in the morning!

3 Choose the correct linking words in *italics*.

1 I wanted to go to the cinema, *but / so* I didn't have any money.
2 It was late *and / because* I was very tired.
3 It was cold, *but / so* I put on my coat.
4 We couldn't play tennis *but / because* it was raining.
5 I invited Sam, *because / but* he didn't want to come.
6 It was sunny, *but / so* we decided to have a barbecue.

4 Look at the a and b sentences. <u>Underline</u> the linking words that join the sentences in b.

1 a He showed me a photo. It wasn't very clear.
   b He showed me a photo which wasn't very clear.
2 a I saw a girl. She looked scared.
   b I saw a girl who looked scared.
3 a I saw a man in the street. He was singing.
   b I saw a man in the street who was singing.
4 a The man was carrying a bag. It looked heavy.
   b The man was carrying a bag which looked heavy.

5 Look at Exercise 4 again. Choose the correct words in *italics*.

1 We can use *who / which* and *that* to write about people.
2 We can use *who / which* and *that* to write about things.

6 Choose the correct words in *italics* to complete the stories.

> Emma was on holiday with her family in a new city, and they wanted to go to a museum. They were lost. Then they saw a girl **(1)** *which / who* was holding a map. The girl showed Emma her map. But she gave Emma some directions **(2)** *which / who* were wrong! Emma and her family found the museum, but it was closed when they arrived!

> Martin was in the city centre with his mum. He wanted to buy some new shoes, so he went to a shoe shop. He saw some black shoes **(3)** *which / who* he liked. They were very expensive. His mum didn't have much money. She spoke to an assistant **(4)** *which / who* worked in the shop. The assistant showed Martin some cheaper shoes. Martin liked these ones, too, so he bought them.

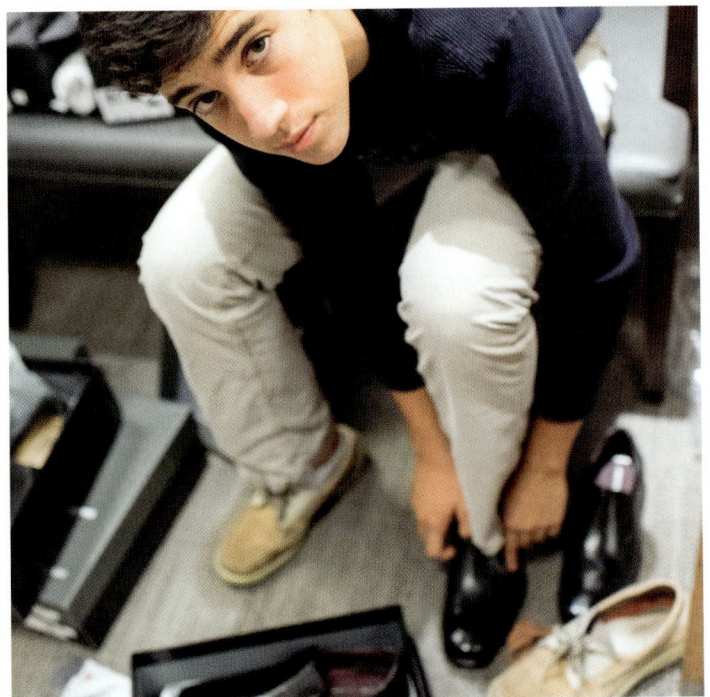

1 Read the exam task. How many things must you write about in your email? How many words should you write?

> You want to borrow a bike from your English friend, Mike.
> Write an email to Mike.
>
> In your email:
>
> • **ask** Mike if **you can borrow** his bike
> • explain **why** you need it
> • say when you will **give it back**.
>
> Write **25 words** or more.

MODEL ANSWER

an informal phrase to start the email

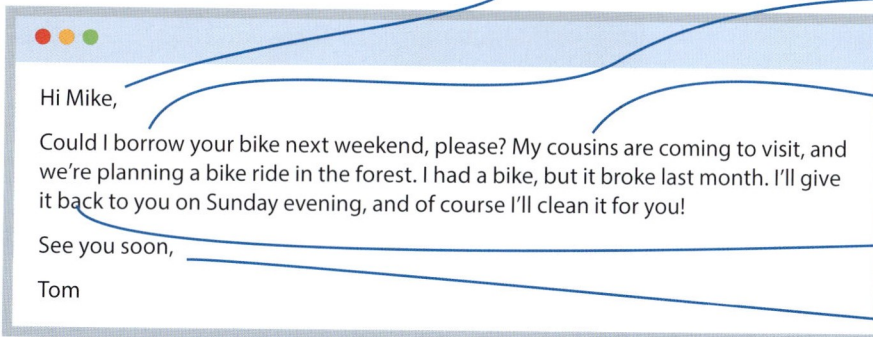

answer the first point in the task

answer the second point in the task

answering the third point in the task

an informal phrase to end the email

Hi Mike,

Could I borrow your bike next weekend, please? My cousins are coming to visit, and we're planning a bike ride in the forest. I had a bike, but it broke last month. I'll give it back to you on Sunday evening, and of course I'll clean it for you!

See you soon,

Tom

KEY LANGUAGE AND IDEAS FOR EMAILS

Opening an email:
Hi,   *Hi Tom,*   *Hello,*

Closing an email:
Love,   *See you soon,*   *Bye,*   *Thanks …*

Inviting someone:
Would you like to … ?   *Do you want to … ?*

Making a suggestion:
Why don't you / we … ?   *You / We could …*   *Let's …*
How about … ?   *What about … ?*

Making an offer or promise:
I could … if you like.   *I can … if you want.*   *I'll …*

Making a request:
Could I / you … ?   *Can I / you … ?*   *Is it OK if I … ?*

Giving good news:
Can you believe it?   *Great news!*   *Guess what?*

Giving bad news:
I'm sorry, but …   *I'm afraid …*

Linking words and phrases:
and   *but*   *so*   *because*

Informal language:
• contractions: *I'm*   *you're*   *she's*
• informal words and phrases: *amazing*   *brilliant*   *OK*

2 Complete the suggestions with the words in the box.

> could   don't   Let's   Shall   Why

1 Why .... we get the bus together?
2 We .... meet outside the cinema.
3 .... we buy the tickets online?
4 .... get the train.
5 .... don't we go for a pizza after the show?

3 Match the sentence beginnings (1–5) with endings (a–e).

1 Could I borrow   a with my homework?
2 Can you help me   b laptop?
3 Is it OK   c your bike?
4 Could I stay   d if I bring my friend Jack?
5 Can you bring your   e at your house on
                            Saturday night?

4 Write sentences about good or bad news. Use the word in brackets.

1 I've passed all my exams. (believe)

   Can you believe it? I've passed all my exams!

2 I can't come to your party. (afraid)

   ....

3 I'll be a bit late. (sorry)

   ....

4 I won the competition! (guess)

   ....

5 Read the email. Underline five verbs where you can use contractions.

Beth's

● ● ●

Hi Joe,

My cousin <u>Beth is</u> coming to visit on Saturday, and I am really excited. She is very good at computer games. I have got a new game and we are going to play some games together. Do you want to come too? I will call you later.

Sam

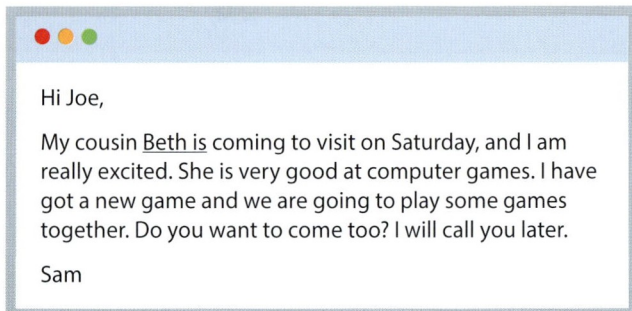

6 Read the exam task. What information should you include in your email?

> Your English friend Laura has invited you to go to a concert with her on Saturday, but you can't go. Write an email to Laura.
>
> In your email:
> • **say** that you **can't go** on Saturday
> • explain **why** you can't go
> • suggest **another day** to meet.
>
> Write **25 words** or more.

7 Before you write your email, complete the table with ideas.

You can't go on Saturday	*I'm sorry, but …*
Why?	*… because …*
Another day to meet	*Why don't we … ?*

8 Write your email, using your notes from Exercise 7.

9 Check your email and make changes if necessary.

☐ Have you answered all the points in your email?
☐ Have you used a suitable phrase to open and close your email?
☐ Have you used a range of language?
☐ Have you used linking words to make longer sentences?
☐ Have you used contractions and informal language?
☐ Have you counted your words?

1 Read the exam task. How many words should you write?

Look at the three pictures.
Write the story shown in the pictures.
Write **35 words** or more.

MODEL ANSWER

A good game

Mark got up and looked outside. He was happy because it was a sunny day. He decided to play football. He then found his football and hurried outside. Next, he called his friends. Later, his friends arrived and they played together. They had a wonderful time!

this tells the first part of the story

past simple verbs for the main events in the story

adjectives and adverbs make the story more interesting

this tells the second part of the story

this tells the third part of the story

KEY LANGUAGE AND IDEAS FOR STORIES

Give the story an interesting title:
The robbery   *A day out*

Use past simple and past continuous verbs:
Mark got up   *It was raining*

Use time expressions:
First   then   later   the next day

Use adjectives to describe people, places and feelings:
friendly   kind   busy   excited   angry

Use adverbs:
quickly   slowly   carefully

Use interesting verbs:
hurried   ran   shouted

2 Complete the story with the past simple or past continuous form of the verbs in brackets.

> **A surprise visit**
>
> Mary was at home one afternoon. She (1) ....
> (feel) bored because it (2) .... (rain). Suddenly,
> Mary's friend Sara (3) .... (arrive) at the
> house. She (4) .... (carry) a pizza in a box,
> and a video game. Mary was very happy! Mary and Sara
> (5) .... (eat) the pizza together and
> (6) .... (play) the game.

3 Choose the correct time expressions to complete the two stories.

> Max decided to make a cake. (1) *First / Next*, he went to
> the supermarket to buy some eggs and butter.
> (2) *Suddenly / Next* he mixed everything together
> quickly and put the cake in the oven. (3) *Finally /
> First*, the cake was ready! Max ate a big slice, and it was
> fantastic!

> Paula was cycling home. (4) *First / Suddenly*, she saw a
> puppy in the road. It was on its own, and it looked sad. It
> was her friend Sam's dog. Paula called the dog to her.
> (5) *Then / Finally*, she phoned Sam. (6) *Finally / Next*,
> Sam arrived. He was very pleased, and the dog was so
> excited!

4 Cross out the adjective that is <u>not possible in each sentence.</u>

1 I was feeling angry / happy / tired / tall.
2 The waiter was very polite / empty / kind / friendly.
3 The town was quite busy / quiet / pleased / old.
4 She was wearing a blue / big / quick / pretty hat.
5 It was a boring / great / high / brilliant film.
6 He was carrying a small / black / ready / new suitcase.

5 Read the exam task. Before you write your story, complete the table with ideas.

> Look at the three pictures.
> Write the story shown in the pictures.
> Write **35 words** or more.

Picture 1	
Picture 2	
Picture 3	

6 Write your story, using your notes from Exercise 5.

7 Check your story and make changes if necessary.

- [ ] Have you written about all three pictures?
- [ ] Have you used past simple verbs?
- [ ] Have you used adjectives and adverbs to make your story interesting?
- [ ] Have you counted your words?

GIVING PERSONAL INFORMATION

1 🔊 46 Listen to two students giving personal information. Complete the table.

	Pablo	**Lucia**
Age		
From		

KEY LANGUAGE & IDEAS FOR GIVING PERSONAL INFORMATION

Saying your name:
My name is / My name's …

Saying your age:
I'm … years old.

Saying where you come from:
I come from …

Saying where you live:
I live in …

2 🔊 46 Match the sentence beginnings (1–4) with the endings (a–d). Listen again and check.

1 My	a in Milan.
2 I come	b name's Paul.
3 I'm fourteen	c from Madrid.
4 I live	d years old.

TALKING ABOUT HABITS, LIKES & DISLIKES

1 🔊 47 Listen to Sophie talking about her habits. Which activities does she talk about?

> doing homework   going to the cinema
> meeting friends   playing football   playing tennis
> watching TV

KEY LANGUAGE & IDEAS FOR TALKING ABOUT HABITS

I sometimes …
I often …
I usually …
I always …
I never …
I … every day / every weekend / on Saturdays.

Use words like *sometimes*, *often*, etc. with the present simple form of verbs:
I **sometimes meet** my friends.
I **often go** to the cinema.
I **go out** with friends **every weekend**.

Notice that *sometimes, often, usually*, etc. come before the main verb, but after the verb *be*. Phrases such as *every day, every weekend, on Saturdays* come at the end:
I **never play** football.
I**'m never** late.
I **often play** video games.
I **play** video games **every day**.

2 🔊 47 Choose the correct options in *italics*. Listen again and check.

1 I *always get up / get up always* early.

2 I *never am / 'm never* late for school.

3 I *usually do / do usually* my homework when I get home from school.

4 I don't *often watch / watch often* TV.

5 I usually play tennis *in Saturdays / on Saturdays*.

6 I *meet sometimes / sometimes meet* my friends at the weekend.

3 🔊 48 Listen to Sam talking about his likes and dislikes. What's his favourite sport?

KEY LANGUAGE & IDEAS FOR TALKING ABOUT LIKES AND DISLIKES

I like …
I don't like …
I love …
I prefer …
I enjoy …
My favourite (sport, food, etc.) is …

Use *like*, *love* and *prefer* with a noun, an *-ing* form of a verb, or an infinitive.
*I **like** / **love** / **prefer** adventure films.*
*I **like** / **love** / **prefer** going shopping.*
*I **like** / **love** / **prefer** to go out with friends.*

Use *enjoy* with a noun or an *-ing* form of a verb.
*I **enjoy** basketball.*
*I **enjoy going** on holiday.*
~~I enjoy to go shopping.~~

Say *I prefer … to …* .
*I **prefer** basketball **to** tennis.*

4 🔊 **48** Complete the sentences with the words in the box. Listen again and check.

> don't   favourite   like   listening   prefer

1 I .... maths and science.
2 I .... like art.
3 I enjoy .... to music.
4 I .... football to tennis.
5 Basketball is my .... sport.

GIVING OPINIONS & REASONS

1 🔊 **49** Listen to a conversation about different activities. Which activity do both people like?

2 🔊 **49** Complete the conversation with words from the box. Listen again and check.

> about   do   do   don't   fun   going   love
> prefer   think   what

Girl: **(1)** .... you like swimming?
Boy: Yes, I **(2)** .... It's fun. What **(3)** .... you?
Girl: No, I **(4)** .... like swimming. I **(5)** .... it's boring. But I love **(6)** .... to the cinema. It's really interesting. **(7)** .... do you think?
Boy: No, I think going to the cinema is expensive. I **(8)** .... to watch films at home. My favourite activity is cycling. Do you think cycling is **(9)** .... ?
Girl: Yes, I do. I **(10)** .... cycling!

3 🔊 **50** We often give reasons to explain our opinions. Listen to three people giving reasons for their opinions. Choose the reason that each person gives.

1 I like travelling because
  a you meet interesting people.
  b you learn about different countries.

2 I don't like skateboarding because
  a it's dangerous.
  b it's boring.

3 I love this computer game because
  a it's exciting.
  b I'm very good at it.

KEY LANGUAGE AND IDEAS FOR GIVING OPINIONS AND REASONS

Asking for opinions:
Do you like … ?
Do you think … is / are (fun / interesting / exciting …) ?
Do you prefer … or … ?
What about you?
What do you think?

Giving opinions:
I think … is / are (boring / difficult).
I don't think … is / are (dangerous / expensive).
For me, … is (fun / interesting).

Giving reasons:
I like … because … .
I think … is interesting because … .

Use *is* with singular nouns and *are* with plural nouns:
*Do you think camping **is** fun?*
*I think video games **are** fun.*

Use *I don't think* + a positive verb:
*I **don't think** reading **is** interesting.* NOT ~~I think it isn't very interesting.~~
*I **don't think** football is fun.* NOT ~~I think football isn't fun.~~

4 🔊 **51** Complete the sentences with your own opinions and reasons. Listen and compare your ideas.

1 I *like / don't* like reading because …
2 I *love / hate* football because …
3 I *like / don't like* shopping because …

AGREEING & DISAGREEING

1 🔊 52 **Listen to a conversation about playing a musical instrument. What do the people agree about?**

1 It's important to practise.

2 It's very difficult.

3 Lessons are always very expensive.

KEY LANGUAGE & IDEAS FOR AGREEING AND DISAGREEING

Agreeing:
Yes, I agree with you.
I agree with you that ...
Exactly!
That's true.

Disagreeing:
I'm not sure about that. I think ...
I don't know. I think ...
Yes, but ...

2 🔊 52 **Complete part of the conversation with the phrases in the box. Listen again and check.**

> agree with you   not sure about   that's true   yes, but

A: I think it's very difficult to learn an instrument.

B: I'm **(1)** ....that. The guitar isn't very difficult, but it's important to practise every day.

A: **(2)** .... I **(3)** .... that it's important to practise so that you can get better. I think that lessons are very expensive, too.

B: **(4)** .... you can watch lessons online and teach yourself. That isn't expensive.

DEALING WITH PROBLEMS

1 🔊 53 **Listen to two conversations. Complete the sentences with the words you hear.**

1 .... that please?

2 .... the question, please?

2 🔊 53 **Find and** underline **the mistake in each question. Listen again and check.**

1 Could you repeat again that, please?

2 Could you say again, please?

3 Can you repeat me the question, please?

3 🔊 54 **Listen to two people talking. What are they trying to describe?**

Item 1	**a** a piece of clothing
Item 2	**b** a kind of food
Item 3	**c** a game

KEY LANGUAGE & IDEAS FOR DEALING WITH PROBLEMS

Asking someone to repeat:
Can / Could you repeat that, please?   Can / Could you repeat the question, please?
Can / Could you say that again, please?

When you don't know the word for something:
I'm not sure what the word is, but it's ... (a sport, a kind of food)   It's something you use when you ... (play football, cook)   I don't know the word, but it's something you ... (wear, eat)
I'm not sure what this is called, but it's a kind of ... (animal, plant, game).

4 🔊 54 **Complete what the people say with one word in each gap. Listen again and check.**

1 I'm .... sure what the .... is, but you often play this on the beach.

2 I'm not sure .... this is ...., but it's something you wear around your neck.

3 I don't .... what the word ...., but it's something you eat.

SPEAKING PART 1

1 🔊 55 **Listen to Ana answering three questions. Does she use full sentences in her answers?**

2 🔊 55 **Listen again. Notice how she adds extra information.**

1 What do you do at weekends?
2 Who do you like spending your weekends with?
3 Where do you like going shopping?
4 What do you like buying?

3 🔊 55 **Complete Ana's answers with or or because. Listen again and check.**

1 I often go shopping, ... I sometimes go to the cinema.
2 I like going shopping in London .... there are lots of good shops.
3 I like buying clothes and shoes .... I'm interested in fashion.

4 🔊 56 **Read Ana's answer to a longer question. Choose the correct verbs in *italics*. Listen and check.**

Examiner: Now, please tell me something about presents that you buy for other people.

Ana: Well, I **(1)** *love / loved* buying presents for people. I usually **(2)** *buy / am buying* presents for people when it's their birthday. For example, last month I **(3)** *buy / bought* a T-shirt for my brother and he really **(4)** *like / liked* it. It's my friend's birthday next week, and I **(5)** *take / 'm going to take* her to the cinema as a present.

5 **Choose the best answers to the questions.**

1 Where do you usually meet your friends?
   a I usually meet my friends at the weekend.
   b I often meet them at the cinema, or we go for a meal together.
2 Who do you live with?
   a I share a flat with three friends.
   b I live in a small apartment in the city centre.
3 What sports can you do in your area?
   a I play tennis once a week, but I can't play very well.
   b You can play tennis and football at the sports centre.
4 What time do you usually have lunch?
   a I usually have lunch at about one o'clock.
   b I usually have a sandwich and some fruit.
5 What did you eat for breakfast this morning?
   a I don't usually have breakfast, but sometimes I have some cereal.
   b I had some eggs and some orange juice.
6 How many rooms are there in your house or flat?
   a I like my bedroom because it's quite big.
   b There are two bedrooms, a kitchen, a living room and a bathroom, so five rooms.

6 **Choose the correct verbs in *italics*. Then decide if each sentence is about the present, past or future.**

I *go* / ⟨*went*⟩ shopping last weekend. *past*

1 I usually *have / had* dinner with my family.
2 I *meet / 'm going to meet* my friends tomorrow, because it's the weekend.
3 I sometimes *watch / 'm going to watch* films on my laptop because I love watching films.
4 I *cook / cooked* a meal for some friends last night, and it was very good.
5 I *play / 'm going to play* tennis next weekend with my friends.
6 I *buy / bought* some new shoes yesterday, and some new jeans too.

7 🔊 57 **Match one piece of extra information (a–e) with each question and answer (1–5). Listen and check.**

1 A: Tell me something about what you like doing at home.
   B: I like watching films, and I enjoy playing video games.
2 A: Tell me something about what you like to eat with friends.
   B: I sometimes go to restaurants with my friends, and I prefer Italian food.
3 A: Tell me something about the clothes you like to buy.
   B: My favourite thing to buy is jeans, because I like wearing them.
4 A: Tell me something about the places you like to visit.
   B: I like visiting places that are near the sea.
5 A: Tell me something about the sports you like to do.
   B: I like playing football. I play for a team, and we have a game every Saturday.

a My team doesn't often win.
b I love swimming when the weather's hot.
c I've just got a new game.
d We went to a pizza restaurant together last weekend.
e I bought some really nice jeans last week.

8 **Practise answering the questions.**

- What's your name?
- How old are you?
- What do you usually do at weekend?
- Who do you like going shopping with?
- Where do you usually meet your friends?
- What did you eat for breakfast this morning?
- Tell me something about the clothes you like to buy.
- Tell me something about the sports you like to do.

1 🔊 58 Listen to two students doing the task. Do they talk about all the pictures?
Do you like these different hobbies? Say why or why not.

2 🔊 59 Listen to one of the students answering a follow-up question. Does she give reasons for her answers?

3 🔊 60 Complete the sentences with the words in the box. Listen and check.

about   agree   do   like   sure   think

A: I think video games are exciting. What do you **(1)** .... ?
B: I'm not **(2)** .... about that.

A: What about taking photos? Do you **(3)** .... taking photos?
B: I often take photos when I'm with my friends.

A: I take photos on my phone. What **(4)** .... you?
B: I like taking photos, too. I've got a camera.

A: I always go cycling at weekends. What **(5)** .... you think about it?
B: I **(6)** .... with you that it's fun.

4 Match the opinions (1–5) with the reasons (a–e).

1 I prefer to go on holiday with friends because

2 I prefer to play team sports because

3 I don't like doing outdoor activities when the weather's bad because

4 I prefer to watch films at home because

5 I prefer staying in hotels to camping because

a exercising on your own is boring.

b you can chat to your friends and have food while you watch.

c it's more comfortable, and you don't get cold at night.

d you can have more fun with people who are the same age.

e nothing is fun when it's raining.

5 🔊 61 Work in pairs. Discuss the summer activities below for 1–2 minutes, saying if you like them. Then listen to two candidates doing the same task. Did you discuss the same things?

6 🔊 62 Practise answering the follow-up questions. Then listen and compare your ideas.

- Which of these activities do you like the best?
- Do you prefer to go on holiday to the beach or the countryside?
- Do you prefer swimming in the sea or in a swimming pool?

PHRASAL VERBS

A phrasal verb is a verb with two or three parts. The meaning of the verb is sometimes different from the meaning of its separate parts. Phrasal verbs can combine verbs with prepositions or adverbs.

This section focuses on phrasal verbs related to four topics: **getting about, in the morning, people and communication** and **other phrasal verbs**.

GETTING ABOUT

1 Match the phrasal verbs to the definitions below.

> come in   get back   come round
> pick (someone) up   take off

.... = return
.... = leave the ground (a plane)
.... = visit someone's house
.... = enter a place
.... = collect someone from somewhere

PRACTICE

2 Complete the sentences with the correct form of the phrasal verbs from Exercise 1.

1   Our plane .... at three tomorrow afternoon.
2   We're away for a few days, but I'll call you when we ....
3   Yesterday evening my dad .... me .... from school in his car.
4   You look tired. Why don't you .... and sit down.
5   I .... to your house yesterday but you were out.

3 Write a sentence using each of the phrasal verbs.

IN THE MORNING

1 Match the phrasal verbs to the definitions below.

> get up   go out   put (something) on
> take (something) off   wake up

.... = stop wearing
.... = stop sleeping
.... = get out of bed
.... = leave
.... = start wearing

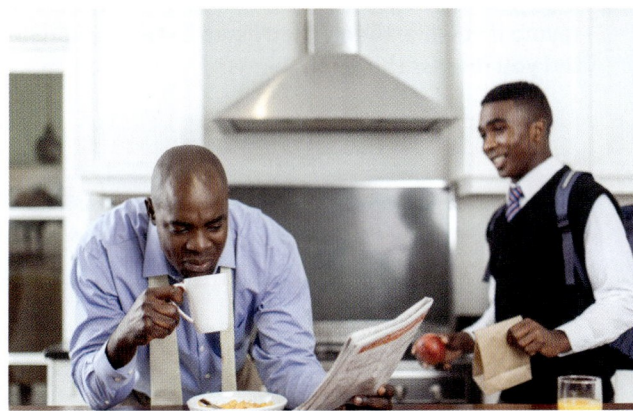

PRACTICE

2 Complete the sentences with the correct form of the phrasal verbs from Exercise 1.

1   I usually .... at 6.30 and then listen to music for 20 minutes.
2   My mother calls me at 6.50 and I ....
3   Next I .... my night clothes and have a shower.
4   Then I .... my school uniform .... and have breakfast.
5   I usually .... at about 7.45 to catch the bus to school.

3 Write a sentence using each of the phrasal verbs.

PEOPLE & COMMUNICATION

1 Match the phrasal verbs to the definitions below.

| call someone back   find out   get on with someone
grow up   look after |

.... = become an adult
.... = return a phone call
.... = get information about
.... = take care of
.... = be friendly with someone

PRACTICE

2 Complete the sentences with the correct form of the phrasal verbs from Exercise 1.

1 I need to .... my little sister while my parents are out.
2 I .... very well with all my brothers and sisters.
3 There's a car outside our house. I want to .... who it belongs to.
4 Sorry, I have to hurry. I'll .... you .... tomorrow.
5 We live in the city now, but my parents .... in a small village.

3 Write a sentence using each of the phrasal verbs.

OTHER PHRASAL VERBS

1 Match the phrasal verbs to the definitions below.

| fill in   give back   lie down   try on   turn off |

.... = usually something you do before you go to sleep
.... = stop a machine or light from working
.... = write information on a form
.... = give something to the person who gave it to you
.... = put on clothes to see if they fit

PRACTICE

2 Complete the sentences with the correct form of the phrasal verbs from Exercise 1.

1 I've got a bad headache so I'm going to ....
2 Don't forget to .... the lights when you leave the building.
3 I always .... shoes .... before I buy them.
4 To get a passport you have to .... a lot of forms.
5 When are you going to .... the book I lent you?

3 Write a sentence using each of the phrasal verbs.

IRREGULAR VERBS

verb	past simple	past participle
be	was / were	been
become	became	become
begin	began	begun
break	broke	broken
build	built	built
burn	burnt / burned	burnt / burned
buy	bought	bought
catch	caught	caught
choose	chose	chosen
come	came	come
cost	cost	cost
cut	cut	cut
do	did	done
draw	drew	drawn
dream	dreamt / dreamed	dreamt / dreamed
drink	drank	drunk
drive	drove	driven
eat	ate	eaten
fall	fell	fallen
feel	felt	felt
find	found	found
fly	flew	flown
forget	forgot	forgotten
get	got	got / gotten
give	gave	given
go	went	been / gone
grow	grew	grown
have	had	had
hear	heard	heard
hit	hit	hit
hurt	hurt	hurt
keep	kept	kept
know	knew	known
learn	learnt / learned	learnt / learned
leave	left	left
let	let	let

verb	past simple	past participle
lie	lay	lain
lose	lost	lost
make	made	made
mean	meant	meant
meet	met	met
pay	paid	paid
put	put	put
read	read	read
ride	rode	ridden
run	ran	run
say	said	said
see	saw	seen
sell	sold	sold
send	sent	sent
show	showed	shown
shut	shut	shut
sing	sang	sung
sit	sat	sat
sleep	slept	slept
speak	spoke	spoken
spell	spelt / spelled	spelt / spelled
spend	spent	spent
stand	stood	stood
steal	stole	stolen
swim	swam	swum
swing	swung	swung
take	took	taken
teach	taught	taught
tell	told	told
think	thought	thought
throw	threw	thrown
understand	understood	understood
wake	woke	woken
wear	wore	worn
win	won	won
write	wrote	written

Wordlist

adj = adjective, adv = adverb, n = noun, v = verb

Unit 1

alone *adj* without other people

aunt *n* the sister of your mother or father, or the wife of your uncle

boat *n* a vehicle for travelling on water

brother *n* a boy or man who has the same parents as you

child (children) *n* a son or daughter, also when they are adults

cousin *n* the child of your aunt or uncle

curly *adj* with many curls (= curved shapes)

crowded *adj* full of people

dad *n* your father

dark *adj* having black or brown hair

daughter *n* your female child

do homework *v* homework: work which teachers give students to do at home

early *adj* the opposite of late

eye *n* the part of the body you use to see

fair *adj* having a light colour of hair

father *n* your male parent

fun *adj* something that's enjoyable, or that entertains you

get home *v* to arrive at your house

get up *v* leave bed after a sleep

go to bed *v* to go to the place where you sleep

go to sleep *v* to start sleeping

grandfather *n* the father of your mother or father

grandmother *n* the mother of your mother or father

have breakfast / lunch / dinner *v* to eat

husband *n* the man that someone is married to

island *n* an area of land with water all around it

leave *v* to go out from somewhere

long *adj* having a large distance from one end to the other

member *n* a person who is part of a group or club

mother *n* your female parent

mum *n* your mother

nephew *n* the son of somebody's brother or sister

niece *n* the daughter of somebody's brother or sister

parents *n* your mother and father

share *v* to divide something between people or let other people use or see something

short *adj* not very tall; not long

sister *n* a girl or woman who has the same parents as you

son *n* your male child

start school *v* to begin the school day

straight *adj* not curved or bent

tall *adj* higher than most other people

tidy *v* to put everything in the right place

uncle *n* the brother of your mother or father, or the husband of your aunt

unusual *adj* different from other things

wake up *v* to stop sleeping

walk to school *v* to go to school using your feet

watch TV *v* to see programmes on the television

wife (wives) *n* the woman that someone is married to

Unit 2

actor *n* a person who acts in a film, play or TV programme

adventure *n* an experience, film story, etc. which is exciting

advice *n* a suggestion given to someone to help them

afraid *adj* scared or frightened

attractive *adj* beautiful or pleasant to look at

be bad at *v* to not be able to do something well

be brilliant at *v* to be able to do something very well

be good at *v* to be able to do something well

be interested in *v* to want to know about something

be terrible at *v* to be very bad at doing something

book *v* to arrange to use something at a particular time

camping *n* when you stay in a tent

club *n* an organisation for people who enjoy the same sport or activity

collect things *v* to try to get a large number of a certain thing, as a hobby

comedy *n* a film or play etc. which makes people laugh

competition *n* an event in which people try to win by being better than others

cook *v* to make food ready to eat

correct *adj* no mistakes; the right answer

countryside *n* an area which isn't in a city or town and has fields, trees, etc

dance *v* to move your feet and body to the rhythm of music

draw pictures *v* draw: to make a picture with a pencil

end *v* to finish or to stop

enjoy *v* to like doing something

glad *adj* happy

go to concerts *v* concert: a performance of music and singing

good-looking *adj* attractive or beautiful

hate *v* to dislike something a lot

horror *n* a film or story which makes people scared

idea *n* a suggestion for something

join *v* to become a member of a club or group

let someone know *v* tell someone about something

(don't) like *v* to (not) enjoy, (not) be interested in, (not) be happy about something

listen to songs *v* song: a piece of music with words that someone sings

love *v* to like something or someone very much

message friends *v* to write texts to people you like

nature *n* plants, animals and birds, not made by people

online *adj* something you can do on the internet

play an instrument *v* instrument: an object that is used for making music, for example a piano or a violin

play computer games *v* computer games: games that you play on your computer

play sports *v* sports: games and activities such as football, tennis and swimming

prefer *v* to like something or someone more than something or someone else

read books *v* read: to look at words and understand what they mean

scared *adj* frightened or afraid

sleep in a tent *v* tent: a structure for sleeping in, made of cloth fixed to poles

spend time *v* to use time doing something

take photos *v* to use a camera to make photographs

terrible *adj* very bad

try new food *v* to eat food you have never eaten before to see if you like it

type *n* a group of things or people that are similar

watch films *v* film: a story shown in moving pictures at a cinema or on the television

well-known *adj* famous

worried *adj* anxious about a problem or something which might happen

Unit 3

add *v* to put something together with something else

arrive *v* to come to a place

bake *v* to cook something in an oven using dry heat

barbecue *n* when food, especially meat, is cooked outside

bathroom *n* the room where people wash, shower, bathe or go to the toilet

bed *n* a piece of furniture that you sleep on

bedroom *n* the room where people sleep

boil *v* to cook something in water

bookshelf *n* a place, often on the wall, to keep books

borrow *v* use something for a time and return it later

bowl *n* a round, deep plate used for soup etc.

bread *n* a food made by mixing and baking flour and water

break *v* to separate into two or more pieces

bring *v* to take with you to another place

burger *n* meat which is pressed into a flat round shape and fried

classroom *n* the place at school where you have lessons

chair *n* a seat, often with four legs

chat *v* to talk in a friendly way

cheese *n* a yellow or white solid food made from milk

chef *n* a person whose job is to cook

chicken *n* meat from a bird that is kept on a farm and lays eggs

cooker *n* a piece of equipment used to cook food

cupboard *n* a piece of furniture with a door on the front and shelves inside, used for keeping things

customer *n* a person who buys something

cut *v* to use a knife to divide something into pieces

desk *n* a table that you sit at to write or work

egg *n* an oval object made by a female chicken, that you eat as food

enter *v* to go into a place

fast food *n* hot food which can be served very quickly, usually eaten without knives and forks

fish *n* an animal that lives only in water, swims, and can be eaten as food

forest *n* a large area of trees that are growing close together

fridge *n* a large cupboard that uses electricity to keep food cold

grow *v* to have and take care of plants

health *n* the condition of your body

include *v* to make someone or something part of something else

jam *n* a sweet sauce made with fruit and sugar

join *v* to go with other people, or to become a member of a group, club or team

juice *n* the liquid that comes from fruit or vegetables

keep *v* always put something in a particular place

kitchen *n* the room in a house where people cook and wash

lamp *n* an object that makes light

living room *n* the room in a house where people sit and relax

look after *v* to take care of something or someone

meat *n* the soft parts of animals, used as food

milk *n* a white liquid that comes from cows

mirror *n* a piece of special glass in which you can see yourself

mix *v* to combine two or more things together, e.g. when cooking

omelette *n* a food made with eggs which have been mixed with other foods and fried

onion *n* a round vegetable with layers, that has a strong taste and smell

potato (potatoes) *n* a round, white vegetable that grows in the ground

repair *v* to mend or fix something so that it is not broken

return *v* to give or put something back, or to go back

rice *n* small grains from a plant grown in wet ground, that are cooked in water and eaten

roast *v* to cook something in an oven or over a fire, usually with fat or oil

salad *n* a cold mixture of leaves and vegetables that haven't been cooked

serve *v* to give food to someone

shelf (shelves) *n* a board used to put things on, often fixed to a wall

shower *n* a piece of bathroom equipment that you stand under to wash your whole body

sofa *n* a large, comfortable seat for more than one person

soup *n* a hot, liquid food, made from vegetables, meat or fish

stairs *n* steps which go from one floor to another in a building

take time *v* to need a particular amount of time to do or finish something

toilet *n* a bowl that you sit on or stand near and get rid of

toilet *n* a bowl that you sit on or stand near and get rid of waste from your body

vegetables *n* plants that you eat, such as potatoes and onions

wash up *v* to clean the plates, etc. that have been used for cooking and eating

Unit 4

boots *n* shoes that cover your foot and part of your leg

borrow *v* to use something for a short time and then return it

bright *adj* strong in colour

cheap *adj* a low price, not expensive

coat *n* a piece of clothing that you wear over your other clothes when you are outside

comfortable *adj* pleasant to wear or sit in because it doesn't cause any pain

decide *v* to choose something after thinking about the possibilities

discount *n* a price which is lower than usual

do aerobics *v* aerobics: physical exercise done to music, often as a class

do athletics *v* athletics: sports activities that involve events such as running, jumping and throwing

do martial arts *v* martial arts: fighting activities, such as karate or judo

dress *n* a piece of clothing which has a skirt and an attached top

fashion *n* a style (e.g. of clothes) which is popular at a particular time

free *adj* not busy

fun *adj* enjoyable, pleasant, makes you happy

give someone a lift *v* to take someone to a place by car

go cycling *v* cycling: the activity of riding a bicycle

go fishing *v* fishing: the activity of trying to catch fish

go ice-skating *v* ice-skating: the activity of moving or dancing on ice

go skateboarding *v* skateboarding: the activity of standing on a board with wheels and moving by pushing with your foot

go skiing *v* skiing: an activity in which you move over snow with your feet on long thin pieces of wood, metal or plastic

go surfing *v* surfing: an activity in which you stand on a board to ride over a wave in the sea

go swimming *v* swimming: the activity of moving through water in a horizontal position using your arms and legs

hall *n* a large room for events; the area in a house that connects rooms

helmet *n* something you wear on your head for protection

hurry *v* to move or do things faster than usual

jacket *n* a short coat

jeans *n* trousers made from denim (= a strong, usually blue, material)

lend *v* to give something to someone for a short time

low *adj* small in amount; not high

offer *v* to say that you will do something, usually to help someone else

pick someone up *v* to take someone from one place to another, usually by car

play basketball *v* basketball: a game in which two teams try to win points by throwing a ball through a high net

play football *v* football: a game in which two teams kick a round ball and try to score goals

play golf *v* golf: a game on grass where you try to hit a small ball into holes using a long thin stick

play ice hockey *v* ice hockey: a team game played on ice using ice skates, sticks and a puck

play table tennis *v* table tennis: a game in which two or four people hit a ball over a low net on a large table

play volleyball *v* volleyball: a game in which two teams use their hands to hit a ball over a net

player *n* a person who plays a sport or game

pool *n* the place you go swimming

pretty *adj* attractive or beautiful

repair *v* to fix something which is broken or damaged so that it works again

sale *n* a period of time when prices are lower than usual

shirt *n* a piece of clothing worn on the top part of the body, fastened with buttons down the front

shoes *n* strong coverings for your feet, often made of leather

shorts *n* a very short pair of trousers that stop above the knees

skirt *n* a piece of clothing that hangs from the waist and has no legs

sock *n* something that you wear on your foot inside your shoe

spend money *v* to use money to buy things

staff *n* the group of people who work in a place

suit *n* a jacket and trousers or jacket and skirt which are made of the same material

sweater *n* a warm piece of clothing which covers the top of your body and is pulled on over your head

swimming costume *n* what you wear to go swimming

team *n* a group of sports people who work together to play sports

train *v* to practise something so you get better or learn something new

trainers *n* soft shoes worn for sports

trousers *n* a piece of clothing that covers the legs and has a separate part for each leg

T-shirt *n* a piece of cotton clothing for the top part of the body with short sleeves and no collar

uniform *n* a set of clothes that people wear for a particular job, or for a particular organisation

warm *adj* quite, but not very, hot

Unit 5

amazing *adj* very good

bookshop *n* a shop that sells books

boring *adj* not interesting or exciting

brilliant *adj* very good

cinema *n* a building where you go to watch films

department store *n* a large shop with several parts selling different things

library *n* a place with a lot of books that you can read or borrow

museum *n* a building where you can look at important objects connected with art, history or science

online shop *n* a website where you can buy things

pharmacy *n* a shop that sells medicine

police station *n* the building where police officers work

sports centre *n* a building with places where you can play different sports

theatre *n* a building with a stage where people go to watch plays

university *n* a place where students study at a high level to get a degree (= type of qualification)

Unit 6

agree *v* to have the same opinion as someone else

boat *n* a vehicle for travelling on water

bus *n* a large vehicle that carries passengers by road, usually along a fixed route

bridge *n* a structure built over a road, river, etc., so that people can cross

busy *adj* having a lot to do

cheap *adj* not expensive

check *v* to make sure that something is correct

coach *n* a comfortable bus that takes groups of people on long journeys

crossing *n* a place where people can go across a road safely

crowded *adj* full of people

cycle *v* travel by bicycle

dangerous *adj* something or someone which could hurt you

delay *n* when you have to wait a long time for something to happen, usually because of a problem

describe *v* to say what something is like or looks like

drive *v* to make a car, bus or train move, and control what it does

expensive *adj* something which costs a lot of money

explain *v* to make something easy to understand

far *adj* a long distance away

flight *n* a journey in an aircraft

fly *v* to travel through the air in an aircraft

heavy *adj* weighing a lot; not light

helicopter *n* a vehicle that flies using long thin parts on top of it that turn round and round very fast

instructions *n* information that tells you how to do or use something

invite *v* to ask someone to go somewhere or do something with you

invent *v* create something new that didn't exist before

invention *n* something that was invented (see above)

lorry *n* a large road vehicle for carrying things from place to place

motorbike *n* a vehicle with two wheels and an engine

noisy *adj* something that makes a lot of noise

park *n* a large area of grass, often in a town, where people can walk and enjoy themselves

passenger *n* someone who travels in a vehicle but doesn't drive

plane *n* a vehicle that flies and has an engine and wings

pull *v* to get hold of something and move it nearer to you

quiet *adj* something which doesn't make a lot of noise

ride *v* to travel by sitting on a horse, bicycle or motorcycle and controlling it

roundabout *n* a circular place where roads meet and where cars drive around until they arrive at the road that they want to turn into

safe *adj* not dangerous (see dangerous)

sail *v* to travel in a boat or a ship

sell *v* to give something to someone in return for money

ship *n* a large boat that carries people or things by sea

spaceship *n* a vehicle for travelling in space

supermarket *n* a large shop that sells food, drink, things for the home, etc.

taxi *n* a car with a driver who you pay to take you somewhere

traffic lights *n* sets of red, yellow and green lights that are used to start and stop traffic

train *n* a long vehicle which travels along metal tracks and carries people or goods

tram *n* an electric vehicle for carrying passengers, mostly in cities, which moves along metal lines in the road

transport *n* a way of moving from one place to another

underground *n* a system of trains that is built under a city

walk *v* to move forward by putting one foot in front of the other

weigh *v* to have a weight of something, for example, 50 kg

wheel *n* a round object which allows a car bicycle, etc. to move

wood *n* material used for construction that comes from trees

Unit 7

art *n* the making of paintings, drawings, etc.

available *adj* something that you can get or use

belong to *v* is the property of; is owned by

cap *n* a type of hat, for example, baseball cap

carbon dioxide *n* a gas produced by people and industry

draw *v* to make pictures, usually with a pen or pencil

drum *n* a round, hollow, musical instrument that you hit with your hands or with sticks

English *n* the language that is spoken in the UK, the US, and in many other countries

geography *n* the study of all the countries of the world, and of the surface of the Earth such as the mountains and seas

give back *v* to return something to someone

guitar *n* a musical instrument with strings that you play by pulling the strings with your fingers or a piece of plastic

history *n* the study of events in the past

instrument *n* an object which is used for playing music

keyboard *n* an electric piano

learn *v* to get knowledge or a new skill

lend *v* give something to somebody temporarily

lose *v* to not be able to find something

maths *n* the study of numbers and shapes

miss a class *v* to not go to a class

music *n* the study of music (= sound that is made by playing instruments or singing)

pass *v* to succeed at an exam

piano *n* a big wooden musical instrument with black and white bars that make sounds when you press them

playground *n* a place for young children to play

put back *v* return something to where it lives

return *v* go back or put back (see above)

sale *n* noun from sell; when a shop has a special promotion and sells things cheaper

science *n* the study of the structure of natural things and the way that they behave

send *v* get something from one place to another, such as by post or email

spend time *v* to use time doing something or being somewhere

study *v* to learn about a subject, usually at school or university

take an exam *v* to do an exam

take your time *v* do slowly; not rush / hurry

teach *v* to show or explain to someone how to do something

trip *n* a short journey or holiday

use *v* to do something with something for a particular purpose

violin *n* a wooden musical instrument that you hold against your neck and play by moving a stick across strings

worry *v* feel nervous / concerned / anxious about something

Unit 8

airport *n* a place where people go to get on aeroplanes

amazing *adj* very good

boring *adj* not interesting or exciting

bored *adj* tired and unhappy because something is not interesting or because you are doing nothing

brilliant *adj* very good

build a fire *v* to make a fire by collecting wood

campsite *n* an area where people stay in tents for a holiday

climb *v* to use your legs, or legs and hands, to move up something

excellent *adj* very good, or of a very high quality

exciting *adj* making you feel very happy and interested

explore somewhere new *v* to go to places where you have never been before, to see what is there

flight *n* a journey you make by aeroplane

funny *adj* making you smile or laugh

gift *n* a present

have a rest *v* to have a period of time when you relax or sleep

hotel *n* a place where you pay to stay when you are away from home

interesting *adj* keeping your attention

journey *n* when you travel from one place to another

learn the language *v* to study the type of communication of people in a particular country

miss *v* to not arrive in time to catch, e.g. a bus or a plane

pack *v* to put things into a suitcase or bag, ready for travelling

perfect *adj* something which doesn't have anything wrong with it at all

present *n* something that you give to someone, e.g. for a birthday

prize *n* something which is given to the winner of a competition

sightseeing *n* the activity of visiting places because they are interesting or beautiful

speak a language *v* to be able to communicate in a language

stay at a campsite *v* to spend a period of time at a place where you can camp

stay at home *v* to not leave the place where you live

stay in a comfortable hotel *v* to spend a period of time at a hotel

stay with a family *v* spend a period of time in a family's home

suitcase *n* a large, hard case for putting clothes in, for a journey

tiring *adj* making you feel tired

tour *n* a visit to look around a place

visit capital cities / new countries *v* to go to places where you have never been before

win *v* to be first or to get the most points in a game or competition

wonderful *adj* very good

Unit 9

actor *n* someone who performs in plays and films

artist *n* someone who makes art, especially paintings and drawings

cartoon *n* a film made using characters that are drawn and not real

circus *n* a show in which a group of people and animals perform in a large tent

clown *n* a type of actor who has special clothes and a painted face and makes people laugh, usually in a circus

concert *n* a performance of music and singing

dance *n* a set of movements that you do to music

dancer *n* someone who dances, often as a job

disco *n* a place where people dance to pop music

drummer *n* someone who plays the drums, often as a job

exhibition *n* a collection of things such as paintings that are shown to the public

film *n* a story shown in moving pictures at a cinema or on the television

journalist *n* someone whose job is to write articles for newspapers, magazines, television, etc.

music programme *n* a show about music on television or radio

musician *n* someone who plays a musical instrument, often as a job

painter *n* someone who paints pictures, often as a job

photographer *n* someone whose job is to take photographs

pity *n* if you say that something is 'a pity', you are sad that it can't happen, or that it wasn't good

party *n* an event where people meet to have fun by dancing, playing games, eating and drinking

play *n* a story that is written for actors to perform, usually in a theatre

quiz show *n* a show on television or radio in which people play a game where they must answer questions

singer *n* someone who sings, often as a job

sports programme *n* a show about sport on television or radio

the news *n* a programme about important events that have just happened

the weather *n* a programme about the temperature or conditions outside, for example, if it is hot, cold, sunny, etc.

timetable *n* a list of the days and times when students have lessons

writer *n* someone whose job is writing books, stories, articles, etc.

Unit 10

activity *n* something that people do to enjoy themselves

autumn *n* the season when the weather starts to get colder, from September to November in the UK

cloud *n* one of the white or grey things in the sky that are made of small water drops

cross *v* to go from one side of something to the other, e.g. a river

farm *n* land and buildings used for growing crops and keeping animals

farmer *n* a person who has or works on a farm

field *n* an area of land used for growing crops or keeping animals

find out *v* to try to get information about something

fog *n* thick cloud close to the ground or sea that makes it difficult to see

free *adj* something which doesn't cost any money

gate *n* a door in a fence or outside wall

happen *v* to take place, or to be done without planning

hill *n* a high area of land that is smaller than a mountain

ice *n* water that is so cold it has become solid

lake *n* a large area of water which has land all around it

path *n* a long thin area of ground for people to walk on

rain *n* water that falls from the sky in small drops

river *n* a long, natural area of water that flows across the land

snow *n* soft white pieces of frozen water that fall from the sky when the weather is cold

spring *n* the season when the weather gets warmer and plants grow, from March to May in the UK

storm *n* very bad weather with a lot of rain, snow, wind, etc.

summer *n* the season when the weather is hottest and people usually go on holiday, from June to August in the UK

sun *n* the large bright star that sends light and heat to the Earth during the day

thunderstorm *n* a storm that has thunder (= loud noise) and lightning (= sudden flashes of light in the sky)

wind *n* a natural fast movement of air

windsurfing *n* a sport in which a person stands on a board with a sail which moves along the water with the wind

winter *n* the coldest season, from December to February in the UK

wood *n* a large area of trees growing near each other

Unit 11

afraid *adj* frightened or worried

angry *adj* feeling that you want to shout at someone because they have done something bad

area *n* a part of a city or a country

arm *n* the long part at each side of the human body, ending in a hand

back *n* the part of your body from your shoulders to your bottom

believe *v* to think that something is true

bored *adj* feeling tired and unhappy because something is not interesting

broken *adj* damaged, missing parts, or not functioning

brush *n* an object used for cleaning / tidying, e.g. the floor, hair, teeth

brush your teeth *v* clean your teeth with a brush

cut *v* hurt yourself with something sharp like glass or metal

deep *adj* high, often used to describe water or something underground

ear *n* one of the two things on your head that you hear with

eye *n* one of the two organs in your face that you see with

face *n* the front part of the head where the eyes, nose and mouth are

fail *v* to not pass a test or exam

feel well *v* feel good and healthy

fit *adj* healthy and strong, usually from doing exercise

foot *n* one of the two flat parts on the ends of your legs that you stand on

frightening *adj* making you feel scared, afraid

glad *adj* happy about something

glasses *n* something you wear to help you see better

great *adj* very good

grow *v* get bigger, develop, become more adult

hand *n* the part of your body on the end of your arm that has fingers

hair *n* the thin thread-like parts that grow on the head and other body parts

happy *adj* pleased and in a good mood, especially because something good has happened

have a temperature *v* to be hotter than usual because you are ill

headache *n* an illness when you feel constant pain in your head

health *n* the condition of your body

high *adv* far above the ground

hold *v* to have in your hand

hot *adj* having a high temperature, opposite of cold

hungry *adj* wanting or needing food

hurt *v* to give pain

ill *adj* not feeling well, or having an illness or disease

leg *n* one of the long parts of the body that is used for walking

lie down *v* put your body in a horizontal position, usually when you are tired or go to bed

(what's the) matter(?): (what is the) problem(?); (what is) wrong(?)

medicine *n* something you eat or drink to cure an illness

miss *v* to feel sad because you are not with someone

mouth *n* the part of the face that is used for eating and speaking

neck *n* the part of the body between your head and your shoulders

nose *n* the part of your face that you breathe through and smell with

pain *n* an unpleasant feeling caused by an injury or illness

piece *n* a part of something bigger

plaster *n* a piece of fabric or elastic to treat a cut

prize *n* something you get for winning a competition or a game

scared *adj* feeling fear; frightened; afraid

sick *adj* ill

side *n* the outside part of something – usually not the top or bottom

sorry *adj* used to apologise when you have done something wrong

stomach *n* the part of your body where food is digested

strange *adj* unusual, different, unknown

sweets *n* food often with lots of sugar that are popular especially with children

thirsty *adj* wanting or needing a drink

tired *adj* feeling that you want to rest or sleep

tooth (teeth pl) *n* one of the hard white things in your mouth that you use for biting

toothache *n* a pain in the teeth

toothbrush *n* something you use to clean your teeth

trainer *n* a person who helps you get better at something, e.g. sports.

unhappy *adj* sad

Unit 12

alarm clock *n* a clock that makes a noise to wake you

call *v* to telephone someone

case *n* a container for storing or protecting something

CD player *n* a piece of equipment for playing music CDs

chat *v* to talk with someone in a friendly way

cooker *n* a piece of equipment used for cooking food

dark *adj* without light

digital camera *n* a type of camera that records images that you can use and store on a computer

download films or music *v* to copy films or music from the internet

DVD player *n* a piece of equipment for playing DVDs (= discs for storing music, pictures or information)

email address *n* a series of letters, signs or numbers used to send an email to someone

follow (somebody on social media) *v* when you receive regular news from somebody

follower *n* somebody who follows somebody else on social media

fridge *n* a place to keep food cold

game *n* something you play for fun, usually with other people

games console *n* a machine for playing video games on your TV

internet *n* the system that connects all computers where you can find websites

keyboard *n* a set of keys on a computer, tablet, etc., which you use to write

lamp *n* a light that you put in different places

laptop *n* a small computer that you can carry around with you

leather *n* a material made from cow skin, often used for jackets, shoes and handbags

mobile phone *n* a telephone that you can carry everywhere with you

mouse *n* a small object that is connected to a computer, that you move with your hand to control what the computer does

MP3 player *n* a small piece of electronic equipment for playing music

nickname *n* a friendly name that other people use instead of your real name

online *adj* describes something on the internet

post online *v* to put a message on the internet

printer *n* a machine to print documents from your computer

screen *n* the part of a television or computer which shows images or writing

send messages *v* to give someone a piece of information, using a phone, email, etc.

sign up *v* subscribe or join a service

skate *v* to move wearing skates (= a boot with wheels on the bottom or a thin metal part for moving on ice)

tablet *n* a small computer that you control by touching the screen

text *v* to send a text message (= written message from a mobile phone)

textbook *n* a book for students which is about a particular subject

use the internet *v* internet: the system that connects computers all over the world and allows people to look at websites

washing machine *n* a machine for washing your clothes

Unit 5

Grammar & Vocabulary, Exercise 2, page 32

1. **A** 1908
2. **B** April 2010
3. **A** 1995
4. **B** March 21st, 1899
5. **C** Monday 23rd March, 1857

Unit 8

Grammar & Vocabulary, Exercise 2, page 48

Look at your answers. Count the number of As, Bs and Cs.

Mostly a: You like adventure. You often try new and exciting things on holiday.

Mostly b: You don't mind trying new things but you also like doing the things you know.

Mostly c: You don't like trying new things very much. You prefer to stay at home on holiday.

Acknowledgements

Author acknowledgements

Emma Heyderman would like to thank the editorial team and Susan White for their work on this second edition.

Publishers acknowledgements

The authors and publishers are grateful and would like to extend a special thanks to Sarah Dev-Sherman (Project Manager - for holding everything together so brilliantly), Alison Sharpe (Editor - for her sterling work in managing the proof stages), Leon Chambers (Audio Producer), The Soundhouse Studios, and Wild Apple Design.

In addition, the publishers and authors would like to thank the following for their role in reviewing the material in general and in particular those who participated in the development of the exam tasks: Jane Coates, Sara Georgina Vargas Ochoa, Cressida Hicks, Judy Alden, Annie Broadhead, Tom Bradbury, Sarah Dymond, Mark Little, Marla Del Signore, Bartosz Michalowski, Catriona Watson-Brown, Alison Sharpe, Sheila Thorn, Lucy Mordini, Trish Chapman, Sarah Curtis, Darren Longley and Ingrid Solberg.

Development of this publication has made use of the Cambridge English Corpus (CEC). The CEC is a computer database of contemporary spoken and written English, which currently stands at over one billion words. It includes British English, American English and other varieties of English. It also includes the Cambridge Learner Corpus, developed in collaboration with the University of Cambridge ESOL examinations. Cambridge University Press has built up the CEC in order to provide evidence of authentic language use to better inform the production of learning materials.

This product is also informed by English Profile, a collaborative programme designed to enhance the learning, teaching and assessment of English worldwide. Its main partners are Cambridge University Press and Cambridge ESOL exams and its aim is create a profile for English usage based on the Common European Framework of Reference for Languages (CEFR). English Profile outcomes, such as the English Vocabulary Profile provide detailed information based on language level and help inform the language that learners can be expected to demonstrate at each CEFR level, offering a clear benchmark for learner's proficiency. For more information, please visit www.englishprofile.org

The authors and publishers acknowledge the following sources of copyright material and are grateful for the permissions granted. While every effort has been made, it has not always been possible to identify the sources of all the material used, or to trace all copyright holders. If any omissions are brought to our notice, we will be happy to include the appropriate acknowledgements on reprinting and in the next update to the digital edition, as applicable.

Key: U = Unit, GR = Grammar Reference, SB = Speaking Bank, ESS = English for Spanish Speakers, WB = Writing Bank, PVB = Phrasal verb builder

Text

U6: Alexis Lewis for the text 'A new type of transport'. Reproduced with kind permission.

Photography

The following images are sourced from Getty Images.

U1: Oliver Rossi/Corbis; Bartolome Ozonas/E+; P Deliss/Corbis Documentary; Jasper Cole/Blend Images; fstop123/iStock/Getty Images Plus; Image Source; Travenian/E+; Sergio Amiti/Moment; U2: Pinghung Chen/EyeEm; Jeffrey Thomas/EyeEm; PacoRomero/E+; Yagi Studio/DigitalVision; Caiaimage/Robert Daly; Jose Luis Pelaez Inc./Blend Images; Kuznetsandr/iStock Editorial/Getty Images Plus; Britt Erlanson/The Image Bank; John Slater/Photodisc; Maskot; U3: Valeriebarry/iStock/Getty Images Plus; David Freund/Photodisc; Carol Yepes/Moment; Sam Edwards/OJO Images; U4: Thomas Barwick/Taxi; Richard Bailey/Corbis; Rayman/Photodisc; Erin Ryan/Corbis; Gen Umekita/Moment; tomprout/E+; U5: Alexander Spatari/Moment; DreamPictures/Blend Images; Jeff Greenough/Blend Images; Compassionate Eye Foundation/DigitalVision; Ktsdesign/Science Photo Library; David H. Carriere/Photolibrary; Grant Faint/Photographer's Choice; Deejpilot/E+; U6: damircudic/E+; Courtesy of Alexis Lewis; Prasit photo/Moment; Laurie Noble/Photolibrary; U7: Fuse/Corbis; yarn/E+; Stock Montage/Archive Photos; Bettmann; skynesher/E+; Letizia Le Fur/ONOKY; U8: SolStock/iStock/Getty Images Plus; Arterra/Universal Images Group; Travel Ink/Gallo Images; Granger Wootz/Blend Images; kroach/iStock/Getty Images Plus; Pavliha/E+; U9: Thierry Orban/Sygma; Image Source; Mads Perch/Stone; Fancy/Veer/Corbis; C Brandon/Redferns; Thomas Barwick/DigitalVision; U11: Lubilub/iStock/Getty Images Plus; Chee Siong Teh/EyeEm; ton koene/Alamy Stock Photo; Francesco Carta fotografo/Moment Open; Ranta Images/iStock/Getty Images Plus; Juanmonino/E+; John Giustina/The Image Bank; FatCamera/E+; yasinguneysu/E+; U12: Bloomberg; Peter Dazeley/Photographer's Choice; Ghislain & Marie David de Lossy/Cultura; Rawpixel/iStock/Getty Images Plus; Reorange/iStock/Getty Images Plus; Infospeed/iStock/Getty Images Plus; Dave King, Andy Crawford, Steve Gorton/Dorling Kindersley; Science & Society Picture Library/SSPL; Marcel ter Bekke/Moment; Cover: Pawel Toczynski/Photographer's Choice; fitopardo.com/Moment; Laurie Noble/DigitalVision; Sir Francis Canker Photography/Moment; vladj55/iStock/Getty Images Plus; EnginKorkmaz/iStock Editorial/Getty Images Plus; Hero Images; Hero Images.

The below images have been sourced from other library/source.

U6: Courtesy of Alexis Lewis; U11: Ton koene/Alamy Stock Photo.

Front cover photography by Pawel Toczynski/Photographer's Choice/Getty Images; fitopardo.com/Moment/Getty Images; Laurie Noble/DigitalVision/Getty Images; Sir Francis Canker Photography/Moment/Getty Images; vladj55/iStock/Getty Images Plus/Getty Images; EnginKorkmaz/iStock Editorial/Getty Images Plus/Getty Images; Hero Images/Getty Images.

Illustrations

Jo and Alina from KJA Agency, Giuliano Aloisi from Advocate Art.

Audio

Audio recordings by Leon Chambers. Recorded at The Soundhouse Studios, London.